"Social impact investing has rapidly emerged as one of the most important and transformational investment trends in the world today. There is a powerful imperative behind social impact investing to fundamentally reshape modern capitalism by harnessing the power of capital markets to address entrenched social and environmental problems such as poverty and climate change. *Social Impact Investing: An Australian Perspective* provides a comprehensive overview of the social impact investment phenomenon and evaluates the many challenges facing the growth of this market both in Australia and internationally. The book provides a unique perspective of how governments can facilitate the growth and effective regulation of this market."

> – **Professor Tom Smith,** *Head of Applied Finance and Actuarial Science,*
> *Faculty of Business and Economics, Macquarie University and*
> *Professor of Finance UQ Emeritus*

"The idea and practice of corporate sustainability is no longer a niche movement. While the concept is gaining popularity by the day, it's becoming more difficult to understand at its core. This book connects all the dots and gave me a greater understanding of the challenges to overcome and opportunities available to build a transparent, robust and effective Australian social impact investment market."

> – **Richard Fine,** *Founder of BioPak*

SOCIAL IMPACT INVESTING

Social impact investing is gaining ground as one of the most important investment trends in the world. While the size of the social impact investing market is still relatively small in global terms, momentum continues to grow unabated. Australia in particular is looking to develop a vibrant and transparent social impact investment market. This book considers a number of innovative strategies and pragmatic policy initiatives that can see the social impact investment market flourish in Australia and internationally.

This book describes how social impact investing can enter the investment mainstream and how a high-quality regulatory framework governing the measurement, reporting and evaluation of social impact will be critical to building investor confidence and ensuring the credibility, effectiveness and transparency of this market. It also examines different approaches to measurement and evaluation that will ultimately be critical to the success of this market. The authors also recognise that governments have a pivotal role to play in growing the social impact investing market, not only in its capacity as a market facilitator and regulator but also as an active purchaser of social outcomes.

This book will be informative for those who wish to learn more about how governments, private investors, investment intermediaries, social enterprises, service providers and other market participants around the world can work together to initiate and grow a vibrant, transparent and well-functioning social impact investing market.

Stewart Jones is Professor at the University of Sydney, Australia.

Helena de Anstiss is Senior Lecturer at the University of South Australia, Australia.

Carmen Garcia is the CEO and Managing Director of National award-winning diversity and inclusion company, Community Corporate.

SOCIAL IMPACT INVESTING

An Australian Perspective

Stewart Jones, Helena de Anstiss and Carmen Garcia

Routledge
Taylor & Francis Group

LONDON AND NEW YORK

First published 2022
by Routledge
2 Park Square, Milton Park, Abingdon, Oxon OX14 4RN

and by Routledge
605 Third Avenue, New York, NY 10158

Routledge is an imprint of the Taylor & Francis Group, an informa business

© 2022 Stewart Jones, Helena de Anstiss and Carmen Garcia

British Library Cataloguing-in-Publication Data
A catalogue record for this book is available from the British Library

Library of Congress Cataloging-in-Publication Data
Names: Jones, Stewart, 1964– author. | De Anstiss, Helena, author. |
Garcia, Carmen (Corporate social responsibility consultant), author.
Title: Social impact investing: an Australian perspective /
Stewart Jones, Helena de Anstiss and Carmen Garcia.
Description: Abingdon, Oxon; New York, NY: Routledge, 2022. |
Includes bibliographical references and index. |
Contents: Introduction – The Evolution of Corporate Social Responsibility Concepts –
The Rise of Social Impact Investing – Evaluating Alternative Types of Social Impact
Investments – International Approaches to Growing and Regulating the Social Impact
Investment Market – Towards a Viable SII Market in Australia – Approaches to
Measuring and Evaluating Social Impact – Epilogue and Future Directions.
Identifiers: LCCN 2021038281 (print) | LCCN 2021038282 (ebook) |
ISBN 9781032126548 (hardback) | ISBN 9781032126531 (paperback) |
ISBN 9781003225591 (ebook)
Subjects: LCSH: Investments–Moral and ethical aspects–Australia. |
Social responsibility of business–Australia.
Classification: LCC HG4515.13.J66 2022 (print) |
LCC HG4515.13 (ebook) | DDC 332.6–dc23
LC record available at https://lccn.loc.gov/2021038281
LC ebook record available at https://lccn.loc.gov/2021038282

ISBN: 978-1-03-212654-8 (hbk)
ISBN: 978-1-03-212653-1 (pbk)
ISBN: 978-1-00-322559-1 (ebk)

DOI: 10.4324/9781003225591

Typeset in Bembo
by Newgen Publishing UK

CONTENTS

ILLUSTRATIONS

Figures

Tables

ACRONYMS

AAB	Australian Advisory Board on Impact Investing
AASB	Australian Accounting Standards Board
ACNC	Australian Charities and Not-for-profit Commission
APRA	Australian Prudential and Regulatory Authority
ASIC	Australian Securities and Investments Commission
ASX	Australian Stock Exchange
AUASB	Auditing and Assurance Standards Board
AUM	Assets Under Management
BICS	Bloomberg Industrial Classification System
CART	Classification and Regression Trees
CEFC	Clean Energy Finance Corporation (Australia)
CEO	Chief Executive Officer
CFO	Chief Financial Officer
CIFF	Children's Investment Fund Foundation
CMAC	Corporations and Markets Advisory Committee
CSD	Commission on Sustainable Development
CSR	Corporate Social Responsibility
CSV	Creating Shared Value
DGR	Deductible Gift Recipient
DIB	Development Impact Bond
DPC	Department of Premier and Cabinet
EEA	European Environmental Agency
EMIIF	Emerging Markets Impact Investment Fund
ESG	Environmental, Social and Governance
EU	European Union
FASB	Financial Accounting Standards Board (United States)
FCA	Financial Conduct Authority (UK)

FSI	Financial System Inquiry (Australia)
G7	Group of Seven includes the following countries: Canada, France, Germany, Italy, Japan, the United Kingdom and the United States
G8	Group of Eight includes the following countries: Canada, France, Germany, Italy, Japan, Russia, the United Kingdom and the United States
G20	The Group of 20 includes the following countries: Argentina, Australia, Brazil, Canada, China, France, Germany, India, Indonesia, Italy, Japan, South Korea, Mexico, Russia, Saudi Arabia, South Africa, Turkey, the United Kingdom, the United States and the European Union.
GAAP	Generally Accepted Accounting Principles
GDP	Gross Domestic Product
GFC	Global Financial Crisis
GICS	Global Industrial Classification System
GIIN	Global Impact Investing Network
GIIRS	Global Impact Investment Rating System
GPFS	General Purpose Financial Statements
GSG	Global Social Impact Investment Steering Group
IAIA	International Association for Impact Assessment
IBA	Indigenous Business Australia
ICA	Impact Capital Australia (Blueprint)
IDB	Inter-American Development Bank
IFRS	International Financial Reporting Standards
IID	Independently and Identically Distributed Errors
IIX	Impact Investment Exchange (Singapore)
IMP	Impact Management Project
IRIS	Impact Reporting Investment Standard
ISO	International Organization for Standardization
IWA	Impact Weighted Accounts
LCM	Latent Class Multinomial
MDA	Multiple Discriminant Analysis
ML	Machine Learning
MNL	Multinomial Logit
NAB	National Advisory Board
NEWPIN	New Parent Infant Network
NFP	Not for Profit
NGO	Non-government Organisation
NL	Nested Logit
OOHC	Out-of-Home Care
OSII	Office of Social Impact Investment (NSW)
Pacific RISE	Pacific Readiness for Investment in Social Enterprise
PbR	Payment by Results
RCT	Randomised Control Trial

ROE	Return on Equity
RSE	Registrable Superannuation Entity
SAHF	Social and Affordable Housing Fund
SARA	Safety and Risk Assessments
SASB	Social Accounting Standards Board
SASIX	South African Social Investment Exchange
SBB	Social Benefit Bond
SDG	Sustainable Development Goals (UN)
SIB	Social Impact Bond
SII	Social Impact Investing
SIMNA	Social Impact Measurement Network Australia
SIS (Act)	Superannuation Industry (Supervision) Act 1993
SITR	Social Investment Tax Relief
SPFS	Special Purpose Financial Statements
SRF	Sector Readiness Fund
SRI	Socially Responsible Investing
SROI	Social Return on Investment
SSE	Social Stock Exchange
SSX	Social Stock Exchange (UK)
SVA	Social Ventures Australia
SVI	Social Value International
TARP	Troubled Asset Relief Program
UN	United Nations
UNCED	United Nations Conference on Environment and Development
UNFCCC	United Nations Framework Convention on Climate Change

1

INTRODUCTION

Social impact investing (SII) is a relatively new concept first coined in 2007 at the Rockefeller Foundation conference held at its Bellagio Center in Italy. The Rockefeller Foundation conference had invited leading investors, philanthropists and entrepreneurs to explore how they and others might deploy more capital to work for social and environmental causes (Rodin and Brandenburg, 2014). According to Cohen (2020, p. 11), it was at this conference that the traditional concept of 'social investment' was replaced by 'impact investment'. The Rockefeller Foundation report (2012, p. viii) described impact investing as involving:

> investors seeking to generate both financial return and social and/or environmental value – while at a minimum returning capital, and, in many cases, offering market rate returns or better.

SII is now one of the most important investment trends in the world today, and its momentum continues to grow unabated. According to a report by the Global Impact Investing Network (GIIN) (2019), the total global social impact investment market is USD502 billion. While the market is still relatively small in absolute terms (about 0.25% of the outstanding value of global equity and bond issues), it has grown exponentially over the last decade. The Organisation for Economic Co-operation and Development (OECD) report 'Social Impact Investment 2019: The Impact Imperative for Sustainable Development' observes that the growth in SII is not confined to developed nations but has extended to many other regions of the world including developing nations. The OECD report stated (2019, p. 33):

> The role of impact investment has become increasingly significant across developed and developing countries, with an increase in allocations across every region from 2013 to 2017. Notably, there was substantial growth in

DOI: 10.4324/9781003225591-1

allocations to developing countries and particularly in Africa, South East Asia and Latin America.[1]

The rapid growth of the SII market in the past decade can be attributed to several interrelated factors. First, the global financial crisis (GFC) (2007–2009) was the most serious economic meltdown since the Great Depression of the 1930s and brought the global financial system to a dangerous precipice (Jones and Hensher, 2008). An unparalleled spate of corporate bankruptcies, which included one of the world's largest investment banks Lehman Brothers, led to unprecedented government intervention into the economy, as well as several government bailouts of large banks and financial institutions.

The passing of the Emergency Economic Stabilization Act 2008 provided the US Federal Treasury USD700 billion to buy troubled assets and restore liquidity in markets through the Troubled Asset Relief Program (TARP). The American Recovery and Reinvestment Act (2009) (the 'Recovery Act') and the economic stimulus packages that followed was targeted at stabilising falling employment levels and providing a range of temporary relief programmes for those most impacted by the economic recession.

While millions of people lost their jobs and homes as a result of the GFC, many notable commentators questioned the Wall Street culture of unfettered greed and excessive risk taking, compounded by poor regulatory oversight and inadequate financial regulation that collectively triggered the chain of events leading to the GFC (Blinder, 2013).[2] According to Cohen (2020, p. 158):

> The financial crisis of 2008, which has been widely attributed to the self-interested excesses of bankers, led to widespread discontent with our whole financial system; in many ways, it opened the door to today's raging debate about the need to overhaul our system, much like the Wall Street Crash did in 1929.

While governments were busy bailing out many financial institutions with taxpayer dollars, it appeared that many senior executives of large investment banks and financial institutions were not being held accountable for the financial vandalism that led to the GFC. On the contrary, they continued to take generous remuneration packages and 'golden handshakes' while their companies struggled or failed. The catchcry of 'private profits but socialised losses' took hold and created a deep sense of distrust and dissatisfaction with modern capitalism and free markets. The system had not only failed but was seen to perpetrate the most egregious economic injustices in society where the unsuspecting public not only had to bail out Wall Street excesses but ultimately bear the brunt of the worst economic impacts of the GFC. The climate of distrust, dissatisfaction and uncertainty with the economic system was an unwitting incubator for new investment approaches, such as SII, which provided a compelling alternative to the status quo by engendering a renewed sense of social responsibility and purpose to investment markets. As stated in the G8 Social Impact Investment Taskforce report in September 2014[3] (p. 1):

> The financial crash of 2008 highlighted the need for a renewed effort to ensure that finance helps build a healthy society. This requires a paradigm shift in capital market thinking, from two-dimensions to three. By bringing a third dimension, impact, to the 20th century capital market dimensions of risk and return, impact investing has the potential to transform our ability to build a better society for all … Doing good and doing well are no longer seen as incompatible. There is a growing desire to reconnect work with meaning and purpose, to make a difference.

Second, as noted by McHugh et al. (2013), the GFC led to greater austerity in government expenditure as the costs of soaring government debt levels and deficits took their toll. While government expenditure was declining, all manner of economic and social disadvantage grew sharply over this period exacerbated by many countries falling into deep recessions. This inevitably led governments to consider more efficient and fiscally sustainable ways to fund costly social programmes, particularly the utilisation of more cost-effective funding models and outsourcing approaches.

Governments and investors started to recognise that harnessing the power of capital markets through SII is a potentially innovative strategy for tackling challenging social and environmental problems. Traditional philanthropy is also important, but its size and scale render it too limited and fragmented to handle the large and very costly social and environmental challenges facing the world, such as lack of adequate education and healthcare, homelessness, refugee crises and climate change.[4]

Even in quite prosperous countries such as Australia, the Australian Taskforce on Social Impact Investing report (2019) contextualised the importance of SII in terms of the enduring social problems of the age including high poverty levels and other forms of social and economic disadvantage. Impact investing was seen as a means by which governments could tackle such problems more cost-effectively and with potentially lower risk for taxpayer dollars. Furthermore, blending private sector investment with social outcome objectives can enhance experimentation, innovation and more rapid learning in targeted social programmes while having social outcomes subjected to more rigorous and transparent performance measurement and evaluation. This can create potentially more efficient and accountable service delivery with improved social outcomes.

Third, concepts such as corporate social responsibility (CSR) and social responsibility investing (SRI) have been increasingly embraced by the business world in recent decades. From the 1990s, it has been commonplace for companies to disclose CSR information and/or prepare separate sustainability reports in their annual reports. Many companies today routinely provide CSR information and/

or prepare separate sustainability reports with varying levels of disclosure. Large investment houses and influential business groups have progressively adopted CSR as an important consideration in assessing corporate risk and future profitability. For instance, in August 2019 (para. 2), the *Business Roundtable*, an association of chief executive officers (CEOs) of the leading corporations in the US, have redefined the purpose of the corporation from the edict of maximising shareholder wealth to a broader focus on stakeholders, implying a renewed sense of CSR and accountability in society:[5]

> companies should serve not only their shareholders, but also deliver value to their customers, invest in employees, deal fairly with suppliers and support the communities in which they operate.

Porter and Kramer (2011) took CSR to a whole new level by introducing the concept of creating shared value (CSV), giving a new meaning to the notion that 'it pays to do good'. According to Porter and Kramer, if corporations can re-align and refocus their business models and strategies to address social and environmental challenges, there is a potential to prosper financially through growth/innovation opportunities in new products, services and markets. Cohen (2020, p. 12) also advocates thinking outside the square of conventional finance and traditional business practices. He argues that impact investing (a closely related concept to CSV) needs to be at the heart of our society and economic system and advocates a fundamental rethinking or reshaping of the traditional risk–return relationship to embrace the new concept of risk–return–impact. Here, businesses should continue making as much profit as possible, but in a manner consistent with achieving the highest social impact within acceptable risk levels.

In summary, SII is gaining momentum because it appears to be meeting a deep-seated investor desire to fulfil a social impact objective which need not be at the expense of making satisfactory or even below market financial returns. Some insight was provided by the GIIN annual impact investor survey (2020a), which included data and perspectives from 294 individual impact investing organisations. In terms of the motivation for impact investing, the top three reasons provided by respondent investors for making SIIs all related to the importance of social impact itself (see GIIN, 2020a, p. xv). According to the survey, most respondents (87%) considered both 'impact being central to their mission' and 'their commitment as responsible investors' as 'very important' motivations. Additionally, the survey indicates that 81% of respondents believed that impact investing was an efficient way to achieve impact goals and 70% found the financial attractiveness of impact investing compared to other investment approaches as 'at least somewhat important'. Approximately 88% of respondents reported meeting or exceeding their financial expectations, while 67% sought market competitive returns for their assets (see p. xv).

In the Australian context, governments at the federal and state levels have shown considerable interest in the growth of the SII market. The Australian Taskforce on Social Impact Investing released an interim report in 2019 which provides a blueprint for the future development of this market in Australia. While federal and state governments in Australia have made varying levels of commitment to SII, the Australian market is still in its infancy, even being referred to as a 'cottage industry' by the Australian Taskforce. Echoing the G8 Taskforce report (2014) recommendations on SII, the Australian Taskforce envisages a critical role for government in growing the SII market, not only as a market facilitator and market regulator but also as an active market participant in the purchase of social outcomes (such as through social impact bonds [SIBs]).

This book assesses the state of play of the SII market internationally and in Australia. We consider several initiatives and proposals that have the potential to enhance the viability, credibility and transparency of the SII market and ultimately stimulate its growth in Australia. We also consider the many challenges and headwinds ahead which include[6] the following:

1. Limited SII investment opportunities available for investors and the lack of expert intermediaries who can structure, coordinate and manage risk for SII funding options;
2. Lack of secondary markets, such as a social stock exchange or social investment wholesaler, to facilitate social impact investment;
3. Small and illiquid impact investment markets with no clear exit strategies for investments;
4. Cost and complexity of SII funding options (such as SIBs) and the time it can take to set up these arrangements;
5. Lack of robust metrics for measuring and evaluating social outcomes; including diverse views from market participants on how to measure and report social impact;
6. Lack of good quality social impact data that can support SII investments and their subsequent evaluation;
7. Limited information and evidence on the track record and performance of social impact investments which is needed to attract investment and build investor confidence.

Creating more SII opportunities in Australia and fostering a more liquid and transparent market to attract investors will require some innovative strategies, forward thinking and strong commitment from all market participants, including government, private investors, social entrepreneurs, service providers, investment intermediaries and other parties. The establishment and development of secondary markets (such as an Australian social stock exchange) or a financial institution dedicated to facilitating social impact investment (such as Big Society Capital in the UK)[7] may be important initial steps to facilitate a vibrant SII market with sufficient liquidity, appropriate regulatory oversight and diverse impact investment opportunities at scale sufficient to attract investors.

Mainstream capital markets generally enjoy a high level of investor confidence which can be attributed, at least in part, to extensive regulation with its focus on investor protection. For instance, the Australian Stock Exchange (ASX) has extensive listing rules which cover detailed financial disclosure and auditing requirements, continuous disclosure requirements, regulation over significant transactions, extensive corporate governance guidance and requirements for the application of accounting and auditing standards. There is also extensive corporate regulation and oversight stemming from the Corporations Act 2001.

For an Australian social stock exchange to operate on an equal footing with mainstream stock markets and with the same level of investor confidence, it will require comprehensive regulation covering issues such as corporate governance, generally agreed-upon concepts of social impact measurement and reporting, requirements for rigorous impact evaluation frameworks and more rigorous risk assessment tools for service providers (particularly for not-for-profit [NFP] entities), just to mention a few considerations.

Public companies in Australia are also required to follow generally accepted accounting principles (GAAPs) and international financial reporting standards (IFRSs). A key measure of financial impact is corporate profitability – this is determined by the application of these principles and standards which are, for the most part, generally accepted across the world. Capital markets have disciplinary mechanisms for companies that depart from these principles. For instance, if a company deliberately manages or manipulates its reported earnings numbers (leading to misleading earnings disclosures), this could result in a negative stock market reaction, a shareholder class action or possibly an intervention from a regulator such as the Australian Securities and Investments Commission (ASIC).

If SII is to enter the investment mainstream, a similar regulatory framework will inevitably be needed to build investor confidence and ensure the credibility, effectiveness and transparency of the SII market. As there are standardised approaches for the measurement and reporting of corporate profits, there needs to be similar standardised approaches to measure and report social impact. Corporate performance is assessed by widely agreed-upon metrics, such as rate of return on equity (ROE), profit margin, working capital, leverage, price earnings, operating cash flow and so on (see Jones and Belkaoui, 2010). Similarly, in the social impact sphere, there needs to be greater consensus on the metrics which best capture impact performance and the standards of evidence required to evaluate the achievement of social outcomes.

Another factor to consider is how the costs of social programmes are to be measured. For instance, in an SII arrangement (such as an SIB), all participants need to know the cost of the social programme. Consider an SIB where private investors fund a social programme and government passes the cost savings back to investors in the form of investment returns and principal payments. How will these cost savings be measured? A social programme may deliver direct benefits but also any number of indirect (or tangible) benefits. Will the cost of the social programme include only the direct costs, or will indirect costs also be included? How will the indirect cost savings be measured and with what methodologies? Currently, there is very little literature available to address such challenging questions.

Undoubtedly, it will take some time to resolve the complex and challenging issues surrounding the measurement, reporting and evaluation of social impacts. Traditional financial reporting and GAAP took over 150 years to develop (Jones and Aiken, 1994). Measurement and reporting standards for social impact are equally if not more complex and challenging. However, on an optimistic note, there are many organisations and networks around the world that are in the process of addressing these critical issues with varying levels of success. This book reviews several of these developments and addresses many of the most challenging and vexing issues facing the development of an Australian and international SII market. We also consider a number of policy recommendations and proposals that can potentially facilitate a way forward for addressing many of these challenges.

This book is divided into eight chapters as follows:

Chapter 2 unravels the complex web of terms and concepts ascribed to CSR in the literature. We provide background and context to terms such as CSR; environmental, social and governance (ESG) factors; SRI; and CSV, as well as explaining how these concepts relate to the broader concept of SII. The concept of CSR is an inherently nebulous and poorly defined concept in the literature with many different definitions proposed. While many more companies are engaging in voluntary CSR disclosures, vague definitions, inconsistent measurement and reporting and selective use of CSR metrics have led to a general questioning of the value of many forms of CSR disclosures. We point out that CSR disclosure itself does not necessarily equate to CSR performance or social impact. We also discuss the empirical research literature on the relationship between CSR and financial performance. While an extensive literature demonstrates a generally positive relationship between CSR activity and financial performance, much of the literature is mired in methodological issues that can undermine the reliability and generalisability of empirical findings. Many researchers have also reported that CSR disclosure is related to other economic factors such as cost of capital (higher CSR disclosures have been shown in some studies to lower a firm's cost of capital) and market value. There is less research relating to CSV activity and financial performance although the limited research available indicates a generally positive relationship – but only in one direction: better financial performance leads to more CSV activity but greater CSV activity itself does not necessarily lead to improve financial performance. Consistent with the general tenets of legitimacy and stakeholder theory, businesses that are committed to CSR tend to do so to show they are good corporate citizens or they are appealing to the expectations of key stakeholder groups – they are in a sense giving away a portion of their profits by investing in CSR activity rather than fundamentally changing the way they do business (such as aligning business activity to address social problems). We demonstrate that social impact is more about the latter.

Chapter 3 discusses SII in more detail and provides several definitions from a number of authoritative sources. We illustrate where SII is situated on the investment spectrum which ranges from traditional investments that seek competitive returns (and with limited use of ESG factors) to pure philanthropic investments which can be described as 'impact only' investments. While many organisations and networks around the world have provided various definitions for impact investing, one of the more useful definitions is offered by the GIIN. The GIIN defines SII as:

> investments made with the intention to generate positive, measurable social and environmental impact alongside a financial return. Impact investments can be made in both emerging and developed markets, and target a range of returns from below market to market rate, depending on investors' strategic goals.

We discuss the notion that there are at least three different elements to SII: intentionality, investment with return expectations and a range of return expectations and asset classes. We also stress that impact investing goes beyond CSR and ESG in two important ways. First, it aims to create a positive social impact, not merely avoid a negative impact. Second, it requires the measurement of social impact which is necessary to assess how much social value has been created from a social programme or intervention. Chapter 3 further considers the factors which have driven the growth of the SII market, including the impact of the GFC, limitations associated with traditional philanthropic approaches to addressing pressing social and environmental problems and growing societal interest in corporate social responsibility. We also consider the relationship between SII and traditional philanthropy. While traditional philanthropy has been a powerful force for good, it tends to operate on too small a scale to be effective in dealing with large-scale social and environmental challenges. On the other hand, SII can potentially harness the power of capital markets to address large-scale social and environmental issues. We conclude that while the Australian government has shown a keen interest in developing an SII market, the Australian SII market remains very small. For instance, there are only 13 SIBs and payment-by-results (PbR) contracts currently operating in Australia, ranging in investment size from AUD5M to AUD14M. Given the growing appetite and optimism for the potential of SII among global investors, we consider the conspicuous mismatch between investor enthusiasm and the actual size of the SII investment market and the specific challenges facing the growth of this market.

Chapter 4 considers the many different types of SII instruments used in practice including SIBs (called social benefit bonds or SBBs in Australia), development impact bonds (DIBs), outcome-focused grants, PbR contracts and incentive payments. We find that SIBs are among the first and fast-growing SII funding models in the world, originating in the UK with the Peterborough prison project. We explain the concept of an SIB which is essentially a funding model that pays a financial return to investors based on the achievement of agreed social outcomes. Investors provide the upfront capital for the social programme or intervention which is delivered by a service provider, which might be a private company, a non-government organisation (NGO) or an NFP entity. The savings generated by achieving social outcomes enables government to repay the upfront investment and a return to investors. Other types of SIB arrangement include philanthropic, public sector and hybrid SIBs. Chapter 4 also explains that outcome-focused grants are provided on the basis that outcomes are identified, achieved and measured. Under a PbR contract, government pays a service provider to deliver a public service based on the results achieved. The service provider is responsible for covering the initial costs of delivering the services. An SIB is merely a special type of PbR contract that enables service providers to access capital from investors upfront to deliver services rather than waiting for service outcomes to be achieved. Chapter 4 explains the concept of a DIB which works in the same way as an SIB but with one key difference: in an SIB arrangement, the outcome payer is typically government; however, governments in many developing countries do not have the resources to fund a social impact investment arrangement. In a DIB arrangement, the outcome payer is typically a private donor or aid agency rather than government. Chapter 4 also explains the benefits and potential limitations of SIBs. While SIBs have emerged as an innovative and cost-effective approach to tackling challenging social issues, their rapid proliferation across the world can be attributed to other benefits including (a) the promotion of evidence-based decision-making through the rigorous measurement and evaluation of social impacts; (b) the allocation of resources to where they can achieve greatest societal impact, for instance, where a social issue is currently unmet by existing government social programmes or services; (c) achieving risk transfer from government to private investors, as investors have the most to lose if an SIB arrangement fails. However, SIBs can also be time-consuming and costly to set up as they typically involve quite complex negotiations between investors, the government and service providers, particularly in relation to the scope of the intervention, the outcomes to be achieved and how impacts are to be measured and evaluated. Ultimately, the success of SIBs depend on how well the funding arrangement is designed and structured including (a) ensuring outcome payment metrics directly relate to intended social outcome; (b) clearly defining the target beneficiaries of a social intervention; (c) identifying the full cost of a social programme or intervention so service providers can price the delivery and investors as well as government can better assess risk and return parameters of the SIB; (d) establishing a methodology for evaluating the effectiveness of the social intervention; (e) establishing a process where all market participants can agree on whether the social outcomes have been achieved or not. We also discuss the academic literature on SIBs which is of relatively recent origin (most academic studies on this topic have been published in the last ten years). While SIBs are widely viewed as a promising financing innovation, the literature is divided over their current effectiveness and future potential. However, given that SIBs are a relatively new phenomenon, we conclude that there is insufficient empirical evidence available to make a full assessment of their future potential.

Chapter 4 also discusses costing issues in an SIB arrangement. While SIBs are a promising innovation that have great potential to power the future development of the SII market, market participants such as investors and service providers require relevant and reliable cost information to make informed decisions about whether to enter into an SIB arrangement or not. We argue that capturing direct cost savings for government is relatively straightforward, but measuring the indirect cost savings associated with the intangible benefits of a social programme is much more challenging and complex. Governments generally ignore the indirect cost savings associated with intangible benefits and just focus on direct cost savings. However, failing to capture the full cost savings, or at least make a reasonable approximation of these savings, can lead to inefficient resource allocation in the SII market. A wide range of methods employed in the fields of economics and related literatures can potentially be used for pricing the indirect cost savings of intangible benefits from social programmes including (a) contingent valuation; (b) revealed preference experiments; (c) hedonic methods; and (d) shadow pricing, among others. In Chapter 4, we suggest stated preference experiments as potentially innovative approach for quantifying intangible benefits of a social programme. Using recidivism as an illustration, we propose an experimental design to identify the strongest and most statistically significant intangible benefits as rated by respondents. This can provide a way forward for quantifying and monetising intangible benefits. Finally, Chapter 4 provides four illustrations of SIB and DIB arrangements in practice, including (1) the Peterborough prison's SIB, (2) the Educate Girls' DIB, (3) the New Parent and Infant Network's (Newpin) SBB and (4) the Benevolent Society Resilient Families' SBB. Most other SIBs which have been developed around the world are based on a similar funding structure. The four case studies presented highlight the underlying complexity of SIB arrangements and the critical importance of outcomes measurement and evaluation in determining the overall success of a social programme or intervention.

Chapter 5 considers international approaches to growing and regulating the SII market, with a particular focus on initiatives from the G8, Canada and Australia. In the Australian context, we consider several federal and state government initiatives to promote the SII market and compare these to other international approaches. A number of federal government agencies in Australia are now involved in various types of SII activity, including Department of Social Services, Indigenous Business Australia, Department of Foreign Affairs and Trade, Department of Industry, Innovation and Science, Clean Energy Finance Corporation and the National Housing Finance and Investment Corporation. Further, as part of the 2019–2020 Budget, the federal government established a Taskforce on Social Impact Investing to examine the government's role in the SII market. Many of the Taskforce's recommendations and strategies from its interim report (2019) are found to be similar to other international taskforces and initiatives, particularly the G8 Social Impact Investment Taskforce (launched under the UK's presidency of the G8). The main focus of the Australian Taskforce interim findings is to identify a way forward for federal government investments in SII, including how SII can provide solutions to address entrenched disadvantage and other intractable social problems. In particular, the Australian Taskforce envisages that government has an important role to play in the broader development of the SII market particularly as a market facilitator, a market regulator and market participant. Chapter 5 further discusses a number of SII developments at the state and territory levels of government in Australia. For instance, the state of New South Wales has a dedicated Office of

Social Impact Investment. We conclude that Australia is in a particularly strong position to grow the SII market if the government's current interest in SII translates into concrete policies. However, the final report of the Australian Taskforce has not yet been released, and this is expected to provide more strategic policy detail on how the government plans to facilitate the SII market in Australia.

Chapter 6 discusses factors necessary to promote a viable Australian SII market. We suggest that in order for Australia to develop a deep SII market with many participants (and on a large enough scale to make difference to society), there is a need for more expert intermediaries that can facilitate, coordinate and structure social impact investments (such as Social Ventures Australia and Social Finance in the UK) and the creation of secondary markets to facilitate SII transactions. One way to attract social impact investors, increase liquidity and access and provide clear exit strategies is to promote a secondary market such as an Australian social stock exchange. We discuss some notable examples of social impact exchange platforms around the world which have been established to provide a transparent marketplace both for primary and/or secondary transactions including information on potential investment opportunities for investors. If secondary markets for SII are to be effective and attract investor confidence, there must be high-quality regulation and oversight, including effective corporate governance and transparency and risk evaluation metrics comparable to listed public companies. For instance, given that government performance payments in an SIB arrangement are linked to social outcomes, one of the key risks for an investor is that the service provider (which might be a private company, an NGO or an NFP entity) fails to deliver on the agreed outcomes. We suggest that risk evaluation tools are therefore essential to evaluate the viability, capacity and quality of service providers (and social enterprises more broadly). Chapter 6 also reviews aspects of the distress prediction literature and concludes that while most predictive models have been applied to public companies, they can be readily adapted to private companies, NGOs and NFP entities responsible for social service delivery. Chapter 6 further argues that social enterprises responsible for social service delivery also need strong assurance and governance frameworks to ensure greater accountability and transparency. Generally, we find that charities and NFP entities are not subject to the same robust regulatory oversight and monitoring rules as listed public companies. We observe that while the governance requirements of the Australian Charities and Not-for-profit Commission (ACNC) Act 2012 are fairly minimal, the Australian Institute of Directors have set out more detailed governance principles for directors of charities and NFP entities. These principles relate to (1) purpose and strategy, (2) roles and responsibilities, (3) board composition, (4) board effectiveness, (5) risk management, (6) performance, (7) accountability and transparency, (8) shareholder engagement, (9) conduct and compliance and (10) culture.

One approach for market participants involved in an SII arrangement to ensure that service providers are meeting best practices for assurance and governance standards is to develop a checklist which addresses how well they are managing internal governance issues. This is considered particularly important given the strong links established in the literature between poor governance practices and bankruptcy/distress risk. A potential governance evaluation checklist could be developed using the Australian Institute of Directors' governance guidelines as a basis. An effective assurance framework provides confidence to stakeholders in the SII market that the service provider's internal controls have been established and operate effectively to mitigate risk and that major operational and strategic challenges have been correctly identified and addressed. There are a range of quantitative and qualitative risk factors available for assessing the overall risk and performance of the service provider. In Chapter 6, we propose to integrate these risk factors into a scoring model or rating system that can be used to assess the overall financial health and viability of service providers.

Chapter 7 provides an overview of social impact measurement and evaluation issues. We argue that social impact measurement is one of the most critical elements underpinning a successful and viable SII market. To use an accounting analogy, measuring social impact has the same significance as measuring profitability for a company. Without robust impact measurement, investors will not have a reliable basis for assessing the risk–return–impact trade-off, and impact measurement can easily fall prey to 'impact washing' (for example, where service providers can cherry pick their social impact metrics or concentrate service delivery interventions on the 'lowest hanging fruit'). While we are still some way off achieving generally accepted standards for the measurement, reporting and evaluation of social impact, a significant amount of work has been done globally. We consider many current international initiatives to measure and rate social impact from various networks and organisations, including B Lab and Global Impact Investment Rating System (GIIRS), the initiatives of the GIIN, the Social Accounting Standards Board's (SASB) framework, the Global Reporting Initiative (GRI), the Impact Weighted Accounts (IWA) initiative of Harvard University, the United Nations (UN)'s Sustainable Development Goals (SDGs), the iPAR Impact Framework, the Impact Management Project (IMP), and other approaches. For example, B Lab has developed a comprehensive rating system known as the GIIRS which can rate corporations and investment funds on their social and environmental impact. B Lab provides the 'B Corp Certification' which singles out companies with exceptional positive social and environmental impact. The GIIN has also developed the Impact Reporting Investment Standard (IRIS) system which aims to provide a common reporting language to describe social and environmental performance with the purpose of facilitating uniform and comparable measurement of impact across companies. While impact measurement is vitally important, Chapter 7 also considers the importance of rigorous social impact evaluation in SII arrangements such as an SIB. We argue that empirical evidence is indispensable in demonstrating that a social programme or intervention has been successful with a high degree of reliability and confidence. Hence, the effect of the social intervention must be isolated or 'controlled' for from other possible influences using randomised control designs. Chapter 7 also discusses some of the literature on how social impact evaluation is being applied in practice, noting that the findings are quite mixed. While robust impact evaluations using randomised control designs are common in the US and Australia, they are less commonly used in the UK context.

Chapter 8 considers a number of specific policy recommendations and proposals, as well as directions for future research to help facilitate the growth of the SII market in Australia and internationally. We conclude that there is a powerful imperative behind SII to fundamentally reshape capitalism and harness the power of capital markets to address pressing social and environmental challenges such as poverty and climate change. We consider a number of specific recommendations drawn from the literature to facilitate the growth of the Australian SII market, including a number of specific policies that strategies that government can drive, such as (a) the establishment of viable secondary markets, including an Australian social stock exchange and a social investment vehicle similar to Big Society Capital in the UK; (b) government or standard setting agencies to mandate that corporations measure, evaluate and report on their social impacts in a similar fashion to the disclosure and auditing requirements governing corporate financial information; (c) government to become an active purchaser of social outcomes through increased outcome-based contracting but more particularly through SIB arrangements; (d) improving the quality of data on social outcomes (and the cost of social programmes), particularly through the interlinking of various government databases, which will help establish better information for investors on impact investment performance and opportunities; (e) introducing tax incentives for social impact investment; (f) providing proactive support for the Australian superannuation industry to be more actively involved in the SII market; and (g) considering the establishment of a federal ministry dedicated to SII which will be responsible for coordinating SII policy and strategy in Australia.

Key points from Chapter 1

SII is a relatively new concept that first found expression in the 2007 at the Rockefeller Foundation conference held at the Bellagio Center in Italy.

SII is now one of the most important and rapidly growing investment trends in the world. While the size of the SII market is still relatively small, momentum continues to grow unabated.

SII is gaining momentum because it appears to meet a deep-seated investor desire to fulfil a social impact objective, but this need not be at the expense of making satisfactory returns.

In the Australian context, governments at the federal and state levels have shown considerable interest in the development of an SII market. These initiatives mirror international developments such as SII initiatives in the UK.

There is increasing recognition in Australia and internationally that government has a critical role to play in growing the SII market, not only as a market facilitator and market regulator but also as an active market participant or purchaser of social outcomes.

Creating more SII opportunities for investors in Australia and internationally will require innovative strategies and forward thinking. In order to grow a strong and viable SII market, it is essential that Australia follow the lead of other countries (such as the UK) and establish viable secondary markets, such as a social stock exchange, and social impact investment wholesalers (comparable to Big Society Capital in the UK).

If SII is to enter the investment mainstream, a high-quality regulatory framework governing the measurement, reporting and evaluation of social impact will be critical to building investor confidence and ensuring the credibility, effectiveness and transparency of this market.

Notes

1 The OECD (2019) report (p. 33) recognises that SII started in developed countries, particularly the US and UK, but has now spread to many OECD nations. More developed SII markets are characterised by many types of intermediaries in operation, such as social investment wholesalers and social impact funds. In developing economies, the majority of investors are international players, with development finance institutions (DFIs) playing an important role.

2 Poor financial regulation and regulatory oversight during the GFC led to the passing of the Dodd-Frank Wall Street Reform and Consumer Protection Act of 2010. The Dodd-Frank Act is the most sweeping regulation of the US financial system since the Great Depression. The main purpose of the Act is to promote greater financial stability, promote greater accountability and transparency of financial system, reverse the perception that some financial institutions are just 'too big to fail' and protect American consumers from abusive practices by financial service providers.

3 This Taskforce was established under the UK's presidency of the G8 under the Chairmanship of Sir Ronald Cohen.

4 According to the OECD (2019, p. 102) report, the biggest social challenges facing developing countries (based on the SDG Index) relate to ending extreme poverty and undernourishment, ensuring basic access to water and sanitation and strengthening access to and the quality of health and education services. On the other hand, developed countries have different social issues. For instance, globalisation, low rates of economic growth, demographic shifts and the increasing complexity of society have created a new set of needs, such as quality care for the elderly, childcare support, crime, housing, unemployment and better integration of migrants (see OECD report, p. 103).

5 This contrasts starkly with the neoclassical economic view of the corporation as encapsulated in Milton Friedman's well known *New York Times* article 'The Social Responsibility of Business Is to Increase Its Profits' published in 1970. In this article, Friedman states bluntly:

> the corporate executive would be spending someone else's money for a general social interest. Insofar as his actions in accord with his 'social responsibility' reduce returns to stockholders, he is spending their money. Insofar as his actions raise the price to customers, he is spending the customers' money. Insofar as his actions lower the wages of some employees, he is spending their money.
>
> *(p. 1)*

According to Friedman (1970, p. 3) corporate social responsibility has no role to play if it undermines the objective of the corporation 'to make as much money as possible … without deception and fraud' (Friedman, 1982, p. 133).

6 As indicated in the OECD (2019) report, the enabling environment (such as a country's regulatory and financial system) is a critical factor in facilitating the growth of the SII market. The OECD (2019) report also noted that many countries around the world still perform relatively poorly on indexes such as the World Bank's Ease of Doing Business and very few countries are on track to meet all 17 Sustainability Development Goals (SDGs), at least according to the SDG Index published by the UN's Sustainable Development Solutions Network (SDSN). According to the Sachs et al. (2020, p. 25), the SDG Index tracks country performance on the 17 SDGs, as agreed by the international community in 2015, with equal weight to all 17 goals. The score indicates a country's position between the worst (0) and the best or target (100) outcomes. Based on the 2020 report, the top-rated country is Sweden with a rating of 84.7%. The US is 31st with a rating of 76.4%, the UK is 13th with a rating of 79.8 and Australia is 37th with a rating of 74.9. In terms of progress towards meeting SDGs, Sachs et al. (2020, p. vi) conclude that Asian countries have made more progress (in terms of the SDG index score) since the adoption of the goals in 2015.

7 Big Society Capital is an independent social impact investment institution in the UK, established by the Cabinet Office in the UK in 2012. It was launched with an initial capital of 600m (pound) which came from dormant bank accounts and four leading high street banks (Barclays, HSBC, Lloyds Banking Group and Natwest Group). Being a social investment wholesaler, Big Society Capital does not invest directly in social enterprises or frontline businesses but through investment intermediaries (such as fund managers or specialist banks serving the sector). According to its website, Big Society Capital has the following mission:

> We work with expert partners, seeking to understand the issues, design and deliver investments and grow market participation, enabling a systemic and sustained impact to improve the lives of people in the UK. We assess our investments on the social impact they will have and the financial returns they will generate. We also look at how they will help to build social impact investment in the UK and bring about changes to the system that can often make tackling social issues feel hard to address.

See https://bigsocietycapital.com/about-us/governance (viewed 5 July 2021). See also https://bigsocietycapital.com/faqs/) (viewed 5 July 2021).

2

THE EVOLUTION OF CORPORATE SOCIAL RESPONSIBILITY CONCEPTS

Introduction

In this chapter, we will discuss several terms and concepts ascribed to corporate social responsibility (CSR) in the literature. We provide background and context to terms such as CSR; environmental, social and governance (ESG) factors; social responsibility investing (SRI); and creating shared value (CSV), as well as explaining how these concepts relate to the broader concept of social impact investing (SII) which follows in Chapter 3. While many more companies are engaging in voluntary CSR disclosures, vague definitions, inconsistent measurement and reporting and selective use of CSR metrics have led to some questioning of the value of many forms of CSR disclosures including suggestions of widespread 'greenwashing'. In this chapter, we will also discuss the empirical research literature on the relationship between CSR (and other concepts such as creating share value) and financial performance and other economic factors such as cost of capital and market value. Consistent with the general tenets of legitimacy and stakeholder theory, businesses that are committed to CSR reporting often do so to demonstrate they are good corporate citizens or they are appealing to the expectations of key stakeholder groups – they are in a sense giving away a portion of their profits by investing in good sustainability practices rather than fundamentally changing the way they do business via aligning business activity to address social issues. We demonstrate that social impact is more about the latter.

Background to CSR

Before introducing the concept of SII in detail, we need to understand the context, background and development of CSR more broadly. There is an extensive literature on CSR dating back at least six decades (see, for example, Elkington, 1997; Carroll, 1999; Andrew and Baker, 2020). Further, N. Craig Smith (2003) observes that the

DOI: 10.4324/9781003225591-2

concept of CSR, or the idea that business has social obligations, is a much older concept than first imagined, dating back to at least the early nineteenth century.[1]

The literature is replete with many terms relating to the concept of CSR such as 'corporate social responsibility reporting', 'corporate sustainability', the 'triple bottom line', 'integrated reporting', 'creating shared value', 'socially responsible investment', 'social finance', 'ESG', 'sustainable development goals', 'principles of responsible investing', 'business sustainability', 'green investment', 'ethical investment' and 'corporate governance' just to mention a few. Several of these terms are poorly defined in the literature, and there is a tendency to use many of them interchangeably.

Andrew and Baker (2020, p. 38) note that even within more specialised fields of social responsibility such as 'corporate social responsibility reporting', there are a myriad of different terms lacking precise definition such as 'sustainability', 'social', 'environmental', 'carbon disclosures', 'accountability', 'green', 'social/environmental performance', 'voluntary sustainability', 'sustainability assurance' and 'greenhouse gas emission(s)'.

Let us consider one of the oldest terms in the literature, CSR. Bowen (1953), sometimes described as the father of modern CSR, defined CSR in terms of a business meeting societal values and objectives: 'the obligations of businessmen to pursue those policies, to make those decisions, or to follow those lines of action which are desirable in terms of the objectives and values of our society' (p. 6).

The concept of CSR gained more traction with the publication of several academic studies during the 1960s (see, for example, Keith Davis' 'Can Business Afford to Ignore Social Responsibilities' published in 1960; and Rachel Carson's influential 'Silent Spring' published in 1962). Andrew and Baker (2020) observe that during the 1970s, environmental conservation began to influence the business and public psyche, partly as a response to widespread ecological negligence resulting from economic activity. In 1970, the Environmental Protection Agency (EPA) was established in North America, and 22 April 1970 was the first celebration of Earth Day. In 1971, the Committee for Economic Development (CED) published 'Social Responsibilities of Business Corporations' which posited that corporations operated 'by public consent [where the] basic purpose is to serve constructively the needs of society' (Research and Policy Committee, 1971, p. 11). The creed of CSR and environmental activism continued to gain significant momentum during the 1980s and 1990s which culminated in the creation of the European Environment Agency (EEA) (1990)[2], the Rio Declaration on Environment and Development (which was a 1992 United Nations publication 'Conference on Environment and Development' (UNCED) also known as the Earth Summit);[3] the adoption of Agenda 21 and the United Nations Framework Convention on Climate Change (UNFCCC) in 1992; the establishment of the Commission on Sustainable Development (CSD) in December 1992 to ensure effective follow-up of UNCED; and the adoption of the Kyoto Protocol in 1997, an international treaty which extended the UNFCCC to reduce global greenhouse gas emissions. The creation of these international bodies and the adoption of various international agreements represented international efforts for setting higher standards with regard to climate-related issues and indirectly to corporate behaviour.

Corporate reporting of CSR activities in the form of separate CSR reports and social and environmental disclosures in annual reports became more widespread during the 1990s. Such disclosures offered companies a forum to defend themselves 'against mounting social pressure to address their social and environmental impacts' (Andrew and Baker, 2020, p. 36) and to demonstrate legitimate CSR initiatives to stakeholders (see Frost et al., 2013; Andrew and Baker, 2020). Even though there was (and continues to be) minimal regulatory requirements for CSR reporting and disclosure (Lodhia, 2012)[4], many large corporations embraced this challenge as they were keen to demonstrate their corporate citizenship credentials to stakeholders. This was seen by many chief executive officers (CEOs) as having positive reputational implications for corporate management, customers, suppliers and employees.

As noted by N. Craig Smith (2003, p. 71), most firms have found the 'business case' (an enlightened self-interest approach) for CSR to be more compelling than the normative case (such as asserting a moral basis for CSR). For instance, firms embrace CSR to mitigate reputational risk or to distinguish themselves from their peers. He states few firms: 'opt the normative case for CSR and assert a moral basis for obligations beyond those to stockholders, at least without also claiming a business case (those that do are mostly privately held)' (p. 71). Emerson (2003, p. 35) also noted

> a significant rise in the number of mainstream corporate CEOs discussing the social and environmental performance of their firms not as a means for advancing PR and marketing campaigns, but as a strategy for increasing the total value of their companies.

Irrespective of the motives for CSR, the trend towards great CSR disclosure is undeniable. According to the KPMG survey of corporate responsibility reporting practices (2017, p. 9), the number of globally listed public companies which have reported CSR information has grown significantly over the past two decades. While only 12% of N100 companies (the largest 100 companies in each of the 49 countries surveyed) issued sustainability reports in 1993, this number grew to 75% in 2017 according to the KPMG survey. Among the G250 companies (the 250 largest companies globally based on revenues), the KPMG survey indicates that CSR reporting grew from just 35% in 1999 to 93% in 2017.

However, it needs to be recognised that CSR reporting is a largely voluntary exercise for most companies. While many more companies are disclosing CSR information, vague definitions of CSR abound and lack of consistent and comparable CSR metrics across firms have served to undermine perceptions of the value of CSR disclosure.[5] For instance, many studies have documented that CSR disclosure itself does not necessarily equate to actual CSR performance, and there is frequently a mismatch between the reality and the rhetoric of CSR disclosure (see Frost et al., 2013). One of the most significant concerns with voluntary CSR reporting practices is the tendency of some companies to 'greenwash' (see Delmas and Burbano, 2011). CSR greenwashing occurs where a company intentionally misleads its stakeholders about its true social and environmental practices and performance. While it is unclear how much greenwashing actually occurs in practice, Gatti et al. (2019, p. 2) provided a review of the CSR greenwashing literature which suggests the practice may be more pervasive than once thought.[6] On the presumption that most greenwashing activity arises from the voluntary CSR disclosure regime, Gatti et al. (2019) suggest that greenwashing could be better mitigated through the use of a combination of voluntary and mandatory disclosure practices.

From shareholder to stakeholder perspectives

The evolution of CSR and the proliferation of different CSR disclosure practices can be interpreted through the theoretical lens of different levels of CSR engagement. To this end, van Marrewijk (2003) describes three broad approaches to interpreting CSR disclosures (see also Ratnatunga and Jones, 2012): (1) the shareholder approach. (2) the stakeholder approach and (3) the societal approach. The shareholder approach focuses on profitability as the key objective of business enterprises. This is well articulated by the famous economist Milton Friedman in his 1970 article in the *New York Times* (1970, 13 September, final para.) who states:

> There is one and only one social responsibility of business – to use it resources and engage in activities designed to increase its profits so long as it stays within the rules of the game, which is to say, engages in open and free competition without deception or fraud.

The stakeholder approach is predicated on the assumption that business enterprises have social responsibilities extending well beyond the profit-maximising objective. Corporations are accountable to a range of stakeholder interests including employees, suppliers, customers, creditors, local communities, regulators, government and other parties. According to the societal approach, corporations are an integral part of the social fabric and are therefore accountable to society as a whole. Corporations have a 'social licence' to operate in order to 'serve constructively the needs of society – to the satisfaction of society' (van Marrewijk, 2003, pp. 96–97).

The stakeholder and societal approaches are increasingly being embraced by corporations and investment managers today. As Davis (1960, p. 76) stated prophetically:

> We can be confident that modem business leadership does have the capacity to deal with questions of social responsibility. Although the next fifty years will bring major social change, business should perform effectively in this instability because it is geared for change. Typically, during the last century it has had an unstable economic environment; yet is has learned to live and

prosper therein. It can do the same during a period of social re-evaluation by developing flexible responses to the needs of society.

A tangible shift from the shareholder view to the stakeholder view is evidenced in changes made by powerful business groups and organisations such as the Business Roundtable which represents the CEOs of America's leading companies who together employ more than 15 million people and oversee more than USD7 trillion in annual revenues. In 2019, the Business Roundtable fundamentally changed its view of the business corporation from a shareholder to a stakeholder perspective implying a stronger focus on corporate accountability and social responsibility:

> On August 19, 2019, 181 CEOs of America's largest corporations overturned a 22-year-old policy statement that defined a corporation's principal purpose as maximizing shareholder return. In its place, the CEOs of Business Roundtable adopted a new Statement on the Purpose of a Corporation declaring that companies should serve not only their shareholders, but also deliver value to their customers, invest in employees, deal fairly with suppliers and support the communities in which they operate.
>
> *Business Roundtable, 2019, paras. 1–2*

The shift to CSR and the stakeholder perspective can also be seen in some of the world's largest investment banks. For instance, a letter to CEOs from Larry Fink, the CEO of BlackRock (2020, para. 8) which manages USD7 trillion in global investments, reflects the growing momentum towards CSR:

> In a letter to our clients today, BlackRock announced a number of initiatives to place sustainability at the center of our investment approach, including: making sustainability integral to portfolio construction and risk management; exiting investments that present a high sustainability-related risk, such as thermal coal producers; launching new investment products that screen fossil fuels; and strengthening our commitment to sustainability and transparency in our investment stewardship activities.

And further:

> Where we feel companies and boards are not producing effective sustainability disclosures or implementing frameworks for managing these issues, we will hold board members accountable. Given the groundwork we have already laid engaging on disclosure, and the growing investment risks surrounding sustainability, we will be increasingly disposed to vote against management and board directors when companies are not making sufficient progress on sustainability-related disclosures and the business practices and plans underlying them.
>
> *BlackRock, 2020, para. 20*

While CSR is increasingly being embraced by corporations and investment houses, it remains an elusive concept. For instance, N. Craig Smith (2003, p. 53) states 'while there is substantial agreement that CSR is concerned with the societal obligations of business, there is much less certainty about the nature and scope of these obligations'.

Several working definitions have been provided by authoritative organisations and bodies. For instance, in 2001, the Commission of the European Communities published a Green Paper titled 'Promoting a European Framework for Corporate Social Responsibility' and defined CSR as follows (p. 6):

> Most definitions of corporate social responsibility describe it as a concept whereby companies integrate social and environmental concerns in their business operations and in their interaction with their stakeholders on a voluntary basis.
>
> Being socially responsible means not only fulfilling legal expectations, but also going beyond compliance and investing 'more' into human capital, the environment and the relations with stakeholders.
>
> The experience with investment in environmentally responsible technologies and business practice suggests that going beyond legal compliance can contribute to a company's competitiveness. Going beyond basic legal obligations in the social area, e.g. training, working conditions, management-employee relations, can also have a direct impact on productivity. It opens a way of managing change and of reconciling social development with improved competitiveness.

What is interesting about the European Union (EU) definition is that it goes beyond a traditional definition to suggest that CSR practices can improve competitiveness which hints at the economic benefits of CSR itself. Indeed, an extensive literature has examined the relationship between CSR practices (although mainly from a corporate reporting perspective) and financial performance (see e.g. Margolis and Walsh, 2003; Orlitzky et al., 2003; Beck et al., 2013). We will discuss this issue further below when introducing the CSV concept.

Socially Responsible Investing (SRI)

Related to CSR is SRI and sustainable investing (SI). While these terms are used widely in the literature, there is no consensus on how they should be defined. However, a useful definition is provided by ABN-AMRO (2001, p. 6), a Dutch bank headquartered in the Netherlands:

> An investment process in which sustainability criteria relating to a company's social and/or environmental behaviour play a decisive role in the admittance of that company's stocks to the investment portfolio.

Canada's National Advisory Board to the Social Impact Investment Taskforce report 'Mobilizing Private Capital for Public Good: Priorities for Canada' (2014, p. 4) differentiates SII from SRI in terms of moving from negative screening to a focus on positive social outcomes:

> Impact investment differs from the most prevalent forms of SRI in that it moves from negative screening (avoiding investments that do not meet certain environmental, social or governance criteria) to investment with the intention to achieve positive social outcomes.

This SRI criterion usually involves a positive or negative screening process in portfolio selection. While SRI uses negative screens in portfolio selection (for example, excluding high polluting industries such as fossil fuel companies), SII seeks out opportunities which actively support social goals (a positive screen, for example, including companies which are having a positive impact on society or the environment, such as renewable energy companies).[7]

Australia's ethical approach to SRI

An example of the SRI approach is provided by Australian Ethical Investment Ltd. (AEI), one of the largest ethical investment funds in Australia, managing AUD4.05 billion for over 57,000 customers (as of June 2020) (see AEI, 2020). The AEI fund uses both positive and negative screens in the portfolio selection process. With negative screens, it actively avoids climate hostile sectors which rely on fossil fuels. The fund also avoids companies that are involved in activities which restrict human rights, exploit workers, discriminate or cause unnecessary harm to animals such as live exports and fish farming. However, the fund uses positive screens to target climate-friendly sectors in renewable energy (solar, wind, tidal, geothermal and sustainable hydro) as well as energy efficiency and battery storage. The fund also uses positive screening to invest in certain health-care companies to enable people to live longer and healthier lives (AEI, 2020). Investment screening is only one approach to SRI.

In recent years, institutional investors such as AEI has moved to active ownership or shareholder advocacy to influence CSR sustainability practices.[8] This also appears to be a core strategy of AEI:

> Advocacy is at the core of our business and one of the ways we live our Ethical Charter. We view active shareholder ownership and advocacy as the responsibility of ethical investors and key to creating positive, sustainable change. The growing collaboration between like-minded groups on key issues will have a dramatic impact on future corporate behaviour and performance in Australia and around the world.
>
> *AEI, 2020, para. 1*

This mantra was also echoed by Larry Fink, CEO of BlackRock, in pushing corporate boards to embrace CSR principles and activity. In his letter to CEOs, Fink (2020, para. 20) reasserted the importance of holding corporate boards accountable for their CSR performance:

> We believe that when a company is not effectively addressing a material issue, its directors should be held accountable. Last year BlackRock voted against or withheld votes from 4,800 directors at 2,700 different companies. Where we feel companies and boards are not producing effective sustainability disclosures or implementing frameworks for managing these issues, we will hold board members accountable. Given the groundwork we have already laid engaging on disclosure, and the growing investment risks surrounding sustainability, we will be increasingly disposed to vote against management and board directors when companies are not making sufficient progress on sustainability-related disclosures and the business practices and plans underlying them.

ESG

More recently, the concept of ESG has emerged. While ESG is a relatively new concept,[9] it is closely related to CSR which is widely considered the precursor of ESG. However, distinctions between CSR and ESG have been drawn in the literature, particularly around quantification. For instance, CSR disclosure is seen to broadly relate to corporate accountability and how a company projects the positive effects of a company's activities on employees, customers, the environment and society more generally. By contrast, ESG is arguably more concerned with the 'measurement' of these activities to arrive at a more quantifiable assessment of a company's ESG actions and risks.

In a PwC report, ESG is defined as follows:

> For many, the term 'ESG' brings to mind environmental issues like climate change and resource scarcity. These are an element of ESG – and an important one – but the term means much more. It covers social issues like a company's labor practices, talent management, product safety and data security. It covers governance matters like board diversity, executive pay and business ethics. Some directors think of ESG as window dressing. But when it comes down to it, ESG is about risk, and it's about opportunity. It's about the ways in which value could be destroyed or created.
>
> *Governance Insights Center, 2019, p. 2*

However, it can be argued that ESG also lacks clear definition and purpose, particularly around measurement issues. The PwC report (2019, p. 2) described the ESG 'disconnect' in terms of a lack of standardised data and general consensus on what constitutes useful ESG and how to measure and integrate ESG into corporate strategy and decision-making (see also Frost et al., 2013):

> A major struggle facing companies in the ESG area is the communications gap between companies and investors on the topic. Many investors are looking for standardized data on ESG that they can use to compare companies. But the types of data that are important to one shareholder may not matter to the next. Even within one investment firm, there may be competing priorities. While the portfolio manager may emphasize the company's ability to make annual earnings targets, the stewardship officer may focus on ESG elements with an eye toward long-term sustainable value creation. Companies, for their part, also struggle with the topic. When investors ask about ESG, a company might point to the sustainability group or officer who issues an annual corporate responsibility report. Those reports often take a broad look at the issue. They might describe employee volunteer opportunities at local soup kitchens during the holidays, recycling programs in offices, or recruitment efforts at local colleges. But these initiatives are not what investors are interested in when they think about the company's efforts around ESG risks. Even if the annual corporate responsibility report includes sustainability data that is aligned with long-term risk management – things like carbon use in energy-intensive industries, employee turnover rates and engagement, or material use efficiency, the owner of that reporting is typically not integrated with core decision making at the company. They are usually not a part of the company's strategy development, asset allocation, risk assessment, financial reporting or investor relations teams. As a result, the company may not have a united message on ESG. And they may not be fully including ESG risks and risk mitigation strategies into their overall company strategy.

While ESG is a relatively new concept, it has gained significant momentum in investment circles over the past decade. ESG ratings and rankings have been proliferated and are now provided by a wide range of data providers (such as Refinitiv, FitchSolutions, MSCI, Sustainalytics, Vigeo Eiris, ISS, TruValue Labs and RepRisk) and are frequently used in academic studies, such as a proxy for corporate sustainability performance and management. While proponents see it as a more structured and measurable concept than CSR, this is notwithstanding that many corporate ESG disclosures tend to be presented in qualitative and/or largely non-standardised formats. This can limit its value to external decision makers, such as investors, and internal decision makers, such as corporate management.

Kotsantonis and Serafeim (2019, p. 51) identify at least four pervasive problems with the use of ESG measurements and data. First, data consistency is a concern as companies can present ESG information in a variety of different formats. For instance, based on a hand collected, random sample of 50 large (Fortune 500) companies, Kotsantonis and Serafeim (2019, p. 51) discovered that Employee Health and Safety information reported in the sustainability reports, was

presented in 20 different ways and 'using different terminology and, most importantly, different units of measure' (p. 51). This presents non-trivial challenges for
establishing comparability across firms. Second, ESG rankings require choice of
a benchmark which boils down to how peer groups are grouped or defined. The
choice of benchmark clearly impacts ESG performance across firms. For instance,
using an all-company benchmark will create industry-level biases (high polluting
sectors such as energy and materials will usually do more poorly than financial sector). Benchmarking a company's ESG performance to an industry peer
group will create more direct comparisons. However, Kotsantonis and Serafeim
(2019, pp. 52–53) note that there can be issues if different industrial classifications
are used to define industries, such as the Global Industrial Classification System
(GICS), MSCI IVA industries or Bloomberg Industrial Classification System
(BICS). Another issue arises if ESG ratings are formulated on a different sample
of companies, which changes the peer group and therefore the ESG performance
ranking. Kotsantonis and Serafeim, (2019, p. 53) note that 'the lack of transparency
about peer group components and observed ranges create market-wide inconsistencies in ESG metrics and undermines their reliability' (p. 53). Third, ESG data
imputation can be a problem. Not surprisingly, there are frequently 'data gaps'
across companies, time periods and particular ESG metrics (this is particularly
evident in small companies which disclose less ESG information). Missing data are
often handled through different imputation methods (such as linear interpolation
or singular value decomposition). While these can have a significant impact on
the ESG rankings, methodological questions are rarely discussed by ESG ratings
providers. Finally, there is a significant disagreement among ESG rating providers
on how to rate a company disagree even more so among companies which provide more ESG disclosures (Christensen et al., 2021). Kotsantonis and Serafeim
(2019, p. 56) argue that this provides 'evidence of the need for not only more
effective disclosure, but also for a clearer understanding of what different ESG
metrics might tell us and how they might best be institutionalized for assessing
corporate performance'.

Towards social impact: creating share value (CSV)

As pointed out by Jones and Wright (2018), CSR implies a 'business case' for social
and environmental initiatives, such as through improved corporate reputation,
stronger employee engagement, more loyal customers and improved productivity.
In fact, the association between CSR and corporate financial performance (CFP)
has been one of the most extensively examined relationships in the CSR literature. Improving corporate reputation, attracting more loyal customers and so on
should arguably lead to more profitable and better managed firms. While most
research documents a positive relationship between CSR and financial performance (discussed further below), a major limitation of these studies is that they rely
on corporate CSR disclosure or reporting rather than actual CSR performance.
Higher levels of reporting on CSR activity does not necessarily mean companies

actually perform well in this activity (Al-Tuwaijri et al., 2004; Clarkson et al., 2008; Eccles et al., 2012).

Demonstrating the link between CSR and business performance has attracted significantly more attention through the popularisation of Porter and Kramer's (2011) concept of 'creating shared value' (CSV). The authors (2011, p. 64) claim:

> the capitalist system is under siege. In recent years business increasingly has been viewed as a major cause of social, environmental, and economic problems. Companies are widely perceived to be prospering at the expense of the broader community.

Fundamental to CSV is a reshaping of capitalism itself. Laissez-faire capitalism has created many intractable social and environmental challenges (such as poverty, lack of adequate education and healthcare, homelessness, refugee crises and carbon emissions) as well as market failures that require government intervention which can be costly and inefficient. This in turn imposes taxes on the community which undermines efficiency and productivity. It makes more sense to align the profit motive of business with social objectives as this can result in less government intervention and more economic growth.

Porter and Kramer (2011, p. 66) outline a vision for the reshaping of capitalism with 'policies and operating practices which enhance the competitiveness of a company while simultaneously advancing the economic and social conditions in the communities in which it operates'.

According to Jones and Wright (2018), the concept of 'shared value' goes back to the idea of the interconnected interests of the business firm and society and was first developed by Porter in collaboration with Nestlé (2010). Businesses obviously do create social value through providing goods and services, job creation, paying taxes and stimulating economic growth. However, Porter and Kramer (2011, p. 65) see CSV as a core business strategy rather than a mere by-product of business activity. They argue that the connection between the business and society occurs at a variety of levels. For instance, social issues are seen as central to a business strategy of value creation in that societal needs 'define markets' and 'social harms or weaknesses create internal costs for firms', through, for example, wasted energy and resources, labour shortages, insufficient skills and reduced health and living standards.

In articulating CSV, three key aspects are emphasised: (1) reconceiving products and markets, (2) redefining productivity in the value chain and (3) enabling local cluster development. By engaging with social problems through innovation in processes and technologies, it is argued that firms can not only increase their productivity but also create new markets and expand existing markets which can make them more profitable. Nestlé (2010; Porter et al., 2015) represents a good example of this approach. As stated by Nestlé (2010, p. 3) in its 'Creating Shared Value Update':

> At Nestlé, we have analysed our value chain and determined that the areas of greatest potential for joint value optimisation with society are Nutrition,

Water and Rural Development. These activities are core to our business strategy and vital to the welfare of the people in the countries where we operate.

Nestlé's (2010, p. 5) overall goals are stated in the following terms:

- *Rural development.* We contribute to what we believe are the five ways to increase farmer income: increasing productivity, growing higher-value crops, using land more efficiently, gaining additional non-farm income and employment beyond farming. Our approaches involve supporting farmers through technical and financial assistance, access to markets, and investing in new factories in rural areas that create infrastructure and employment.
- *Water and environmental sustainability.* In our operations, we strive to continuously improve our operational efficiency and environmental performance and apply a life cycle approach to assess our own operations and those associated with the wider value chain, to produce tasty, nutritious food and beverages with the lightest environmental footprint. We aim to provide all Nestlé employees with a professional, healthy and inspiring working environment that fosters personal accomplishment and team development, and that respects diversity and equality.
- *Nutrition.* Using science-based solutions, we seek to improve quality of life through food and diet, contributing to the health and wellbeing of consumers, including those with specific nutritional needs and those at the base of the income pyramid through products with higher nutritional value at affordable prices. We also aim to generate greater awareness, knowledge and understanding among consumers through clear, responsible communication.

Nestlé is an example of a company which has addressed important social needs through innovation while at the same time creating new processes, products and markets (Jones and Wright, 2018).

Despite the popularity and influence of the CSV concept in recent years, the approach is not without critics (see Beschorner, 2013; Crane et al., 2014). For instance, Paramanand (2013, p. 4) argued that the CSV concept is not fundamentally new, although Porter and Kramer (2011) may have successfully repurposed and marketed the concept well:

> There are already several well-written case studies that demonstrate close collaboration between business and communities and that the celebrated strategy gurus are adding little new value. That Porter and Kramer are late bloomers to this field and their blitz about CSV idea as if it was like Newton discovering gravity has drawn a lot of smirk.

Other issues concern the relationship between CSV with CSR. With the exception of the environment, Porter and Kramer (2011) see sustainability as a poorly defined concept. While they position CSV at centre stage, proponents of CSR see it as the ultimate form or manifestation of CSV. In other words, CSV focuses on the here and now, whereas CSR focuses more on the future costs or value of doing business. Porter and Kramer (2011) emphasise a distinction between CSR disclosures and sustainability, with their focus on value creation, which involves innovation, corporate profitability and competitiveness. In particular, the focus on value creation stresses the need to demonstrate economic and societal benefits relative to the cost of various corporate activities in the social arena. Here, Cohen (2020, p. 93) provides a useful distinction between CSR and CSV:

> Businesses that take CSR seriously generally do so to demonstrate corporate citizenship – they are giving away a portion of their profits rather than fundamentally changing the way they do business. Businesses that are seeking to integrate impact generally start by examining their products and services or the environmental effects of their operations. The most advanced are moving to embed impact throughout their whole business, setting measurable impact targets against defined benchmarks to move their businesses away from generating negative impact and focusing on increasing their positive impact.

As suggested above, an interesting empirical question remains whether CSR and CSV are actually profitable strategies for companies. The link between CSR and CFP has been intensely researched (Shinwell and Shamir, 2018), with most studies indicating a generally positive relationship between CSR and CFP, although the magnitude of this relationship, and whether there is any underlying cause and effect relationship, is generally open to question. In a review of 30 years of empirical research, Orlitzky et al. (2003) found a generally positive CSR and CFP relationship. This held true across industries and different study contexts, although the relationship varied from highly positive to modestly positive 'because of contingencies, such as reputation effects, market measures of CFP, or CSR disclosures' (p. 423). Although Margolis et al. (2007) and Joshua et al. (2008) found a more limited CSR–CFP relationship, they suggest the link is more convincing when financial performance is modelled to predict future CSR activity, rather than when CSR activity is used to predict financial performance (see also Beck et al., 2018; Jones and Wright, 2018).

Beck et al. (2018) examined the CSR–CFP relationship by improving on methodological limitations of previous literature. Beck et al. (2018) enhanced the literature in the following ways: (1) by including a cross-country analysis of reporting practices; (2) using a globally accepted sustainability reporting framework to measure CSR engagement in terms of disclosure; (3) the use of quantifiable, third-party authenticated CSR performance information; (4) the use of more clearly specified control variables; and (5) use of a more robust regression framework. Previous research on the CSR–CFP relationship has relied on standard form regression models that can be highly susceptible to violation of statistical assumptions (such as identical and independently distributed errors or IIDs), which can significantly affect the interpretation of empirical results. To deal with this concern, Beck et al. (2018) used the linear mixed effects (LMEs) model to analyse and interpret empirical findings, which is more robust to violation of various statistical assumptions.

The study used a sample of 116 sampled firms, 40 of which were listed on the Australian Stock Exchange (ASX), 38 on the London Financial Times Stock Exchange (FTSE), and 38 on the Hong Kong Stock Exchange (HKSE). To collect CSR data, the sampled firms' websites were accessed, and all published English language reports for 2012 were downloaded. Most of the CSR disclosures of companies were found in stand-alone CSRs. Following the initial screen and analysis, each report's content was hand collected and then coded against all 123 indicators of the G3.1. The authors found that while there was variation in the CSR reporting practices across industries and national reporting jurisdictions, the total CSR engagement was positively and significantly associated with financial performance, 'even after controlling for our CSR performance proxy, industry-level fixed effects, country-level fixed effects, firm size, financial risk and type of assurance provider (i.e. whether a Big4 accounting firm or some other provider)' (pp. 530–531). The authors concluded that larger and more profitable firms with better actual CSR performance, lower financial risk and who use a Big 4 audit firm to assure CSR disclosures demonstrated significantly higher CSR engagement overall.[10]

The CSR relationship has also been examined in other economic contexts. For instance, a report by Clark et al. (2015), published by the University of Oxford and Arabesque Partners, examined the relationship between CSR and cost of capital. Cost of capital is a widely used proxy for market perceptions of risk. Firms with less perceived risk can borrow at lower cost. Based on more than 200 academic studies, industry reports, newspaper articles and books, Clark et al. (2015, p. 9) found that 90% of the studies showed that sound sustainability standards lowers a firm's cost of capital.[11]

A much smaller number of studies have examined the CFP–CSV relationship. Jones and Wright (2018) explored Porter and Kramer's (2011) concept of 'creating shared value' (CSV) and tested the proposition that companies which adopt CSV experience superior financial performance. One of the key assumptions of the CSV concept is that companies will benefit economically through engaging in CSV activity. Jones and Wright tested this empirically by developing a proxy measure of CSV activity based on 26 sustainability performance indicators drawn from a customised database provided by the Centre for Australian Ethical Research (CAER). The authors constructed the proxy for the ASX 300 in Australia over a five-year period (2008–2012). They reported a statistically significant association between the CSV proxy and a broad range of financial performance indicators, such as cash flow returns, leverage, sales turnover and return on assets. These companies also tend to be larger (market capitalisation was a significant variable in the analysis) and have higher growth opportunities. An important finding was that statistical tests of causality (using Granger tests) suggest that better financial performance actually drives greater CSV activity, rather than CSV activity itself leading to better financial outcomes for the sampled companies. This suggests that successful and well-managed companies may well be adopting CSV-related activities as a response to 'management fashions' rather than their anticipated contributions to financial performance.

The vast majority of CSR–CFP studies have examined the external reporting context for CSR information. There are relatively few empirical studies which have examined the use of CSR information for internal decision-making. Frost et al. (2013) provided a detailed analysis of how organisations use sustainability for *internal* reporting purposes based on nearly 100 personal interviews with accountants, directors, CEOs, chief financial officers (CFOs) and other senior managers. Their study concentrated on five Australian entities considered leaders in sustainability reporting and/or management. While the actual names of companies were kept anonymous, the companies included (1) a large multinational finance company named 'Green Insurer'. This company was in the top 40 of listed companies in Australia at the time of the interviews. The company was selected because it evidenced a strong commitment to the Global Reporting Initiative (GRI) framework and the disclosure of various types of sustainability performance information; (2) a manufacturing/pharmaceutical company named 'Herbal Life', which was middle-tier-listed Australian company. While the company had a strong reputation for social responsibility, it provided quite limited sustainability information in its annual report; (3) a local government authority named 'Local Leader' known for its leadership in sustainability management and reporting; (4) a water authority named 'Clear Water' which, at the time of the interviews, was an entity that maintained the water authority for several million people and known for the quality of its sustainability reporting; (5) a construction/mining entity named 'Infrastructure' which was an unlisted subsidiary of a multinational corporation based in Europe. This subsidiary entity was also well known at the time for its commitment to sustainability and sustainability reporting. The interviews were all semi-structured and focused particular attention on the entity's sustainability management systems. Most of the interview questions were concentrated on how sustainability information was collected and reported, the various types of sustainability data collected, how sustainability data were measured and reported within these organisations, the type of information systems that were used to collect and analyse sustainability data, the timing and frequency of sustainability of reporting, the role of sustainability in internal decision-making, how well sustainability data were integrated within the organisation's internal accounting systems and the auditing and assurance of sustainability data. The interview data indicated that all organisations were strongly committed to sustainability and all had 'adopted a variety of significant sustainability innovations, practices and strategies', partly because it sends the right signal to stakeholders (p. 191). Also many organisations were using or had access to quite sophisticated information systems that were used to collect and analyse sustainability information within the organisation.

However, beyond that, Frost et al. (2013, pp. 192–196) identified a significant gap between the external reporting of CSR information and their internal management practices and systems necessary to support comprehensive and reliable measurement and disclosure. Frost et al. (2013) also find evidence of a significant rift between the external rhetoric of sustainability and the internal management processes and culture of some of these organisations (i.e. how CSR is actually viewed and used for decision-making within the organisation). For instance, the interview evidence indicated that while these organisations took a strong public stance on CSR in the annual report (and sustainability reports where applicable), internally CSR information was generally not collected, measured or reported comprehensively nor integrated into the organisation's financial decision-making framework. Importantly, Frost et al. (2013) observe that one of the most critical factors for sustainability information to be successfully integrated for decision-making within organisations, cultural change at the organisational level would be essential. They conclude (p. 195) 'development of a sustainability culture is best achieved through leadership or through embedding sustainability metrics in formal performance management practices'.

Having provided a background to CSR and related concepts, Chapter 3 discusses the SII concept in more detail.

Key points from Chapter 2

The literature is replete with many terms relating to the concept of CSR. Understanding the similarities and differences between these terms provides important background for understanding and appreciating the SII concept.

While CSR is an inherently nebulous and poorly defined concept, many definitions have been proposed by academics and authoritative organisations around the world.

Although many more companies are joining the CSR bandwagon, particularly through increased CSR disclosures, vague definitions of CSR performance and lack of meaningful metrics have led to some questioning of the value of CSR disclosures. CSR disclosure does not necessarily equate to CSR performance and is often used to demonstrate corporate citizenship rather than to measure social impact.

There are three broad theoretical approaches to interpreting CSR: the shareholder approach, the stakeholder approach and the societal approach. The stakeholder and societal approaches have now become more mainstream in the business world.

A tangible shift from the shareholder view (i.e. corporations exist to maximise shareholder wealth) to the stakeholder view is evidenced in changes made by powerful business groups and organisations such as the Business Roundtable which in 2019, fundamentally altered its view of the business corporation from a shareholder to a stakeholder perspective.

SRI differs from CSR and SII because it usually involves a positive or negative screening process in portfolio selection. More recently, terms such as ESG have emerged and is closely related to CSR.

CSV is a relatively new concept related to SII. Porter and Kramer (2011) argue that by engaging with social problems through innovation in processes and technologies, businesses can not only increase their productivity but also create new markets and expand existing markets which can make them more profitable.

There is a strong body of empirical research demonstrating a generally positive relationship between CSR activity and financial performance (including lowering of a firm's cost of capital). There is less research relating to CSV activity although what is available indicates a generally positive relationship – but only in one direction: better financial performance leads to more CSV activity, but greater CSV activity does not necessarily lead to improve financial performance.

Businesses that take CSR seriously generally do so to show they are good corporate citizens – they are giving away a portion of their profits by investing in sustainability practices rather than fundamentally changing the way they do business. Social impact is more about the latter.

Notes

1 For instance, N. Craig Smith (2003, p. 52) states:

> In Britain, visionary business leaders in the aftermath of the Industrial Revolution built factory towns – such as Bourneville (founded by George Cadbury in 1879) and Port Sunlight (founded by William Lever in 1888 and named after the brand of soap made there) – that were intended to provide workers and their families with housing and other amenities when many parts of the newly industrialized cities were slums.

2 According to its website, the European Environment Agency

> provides sound, independent information on the environment for those involved in developing, adopting, implementing and evaluating environmental policy, and also the general public. In close collaboration with the European Environmental Information and Observation Network (Eionet) and its 32 member countries, the EEA gathers data and produces assessments on a wide range of topics related to the environment.

See www.eea.europa.eu/about-us (viewed 5 July 2021).

3 The Rio Declaration consisted of 27 principles which served to guide countries in future sustainable development. The Rio Declaration was signed by over 175 countries (see www.un.org/en/development/desa/population/migration/generalassembly/docs/globalcompact/A_CONF.151_26_Vol.I_Declaration.pdf (viewed 5 July 2021).

4 The Corporations and Markets Advisory Committee defines a socially responsible company as one which '… operates in an open and accountable manner, uses its resources for productive ends, complies with relevant regulatory requirements and acknowledges and takes responsibility for the consequences of its actions'. (A review of relevant reporting regulation is provided by Overland (2007) in her article 'Corporate social responsibility in context: the case for compulsory sustainability disclosure for listed public companies in Australia?' *Macquarie Journal of International and Comparative Environmental Law*, 4(2).

5 The problems with CSR definitions were recognised as early as 1960 by Davis (1960) who highlighted the difficulties with applying rigorous definitions. He stated: 'Social

responsibility is a nebulous idea and, hence, is defined in various ways' (1960, p. 70). While reaching for a definition, CSR is still defined somewhat vaguely by Davis in the context of 'socio-economic and socio-human obligations to others' (p. 71).

6 Delmas and Burbano (2011, p. 65) observed an increasing trend of 'greenwashing' which they define as the intersection of two firm behaviours: 'poor environmental perform-ance and positive communication about environmental performance'. Their sample was based on 'brown firms' or environmental polluters and capture the mismatch between environmental communications (which are fluid and can be changed relatively easily by the firm) and performance (which cannot be changed quickly). In particular, they identify the drivers of greenwashing which include (1) external factors, such as market and non-market participants; (2) organisational drivers, such as firm incentive struc-ture and the organisation's ethical culture; and (3) individual-level drivers which include narrow decision framing and optimistic bias. While 'greenwashing' is suspected to be quite prevalent, it needs to be acknowledged that the empirical literature is somewhat mixed. For instance, Mahoney et al. (2013) find more evidence that the voluntary dis-closure of separate CSR reports by companies is driven by their signal hypothesis (i.e. communicating superior social and environmental performance to stakeholders) rather than greenwashing. Furthermore, Clarkson (2011) examined the academic literature on the value relevance of environmental performance and notes that that the relationship between environmental disclosure and performance is generally positive, despite some mixed results in the literature.

7 While Ormiston et al. (2015) see impact investing as an evolution from socially respon-sible investment concepts, there are also some clear overlaps between the concepts of responsible investing and impact investing. While it is clear the mere act of screening investments does not explicitly generate measurable social impacts, socially responsible investment also includes practices of investing in disadvantaged local communities and social venture capital funding. Ormiston et al. (2015, p. 353) argue

> In these instances, impact investment and socially responsible investment occupy the same space, as investment into disadvantaged communities to combat social exclusion is a strategy employed by the fields of community development finance and microfinance, both of which are subsets of impact investment.

8 Majoch et al. (2012) review the literature on shareholder advocacy, particularly as it relates to ESG performance. They observe that shareholder activism is a strongly growing trend, extending well beyond good corporate governance practices to include broader social and environmental issues. The literature also indicates that shareholder advocacy is an effective means to bring CSR issues to the attention of corporate boards and as well as facilitating the resolution of such issues. The authors propose a theoretical model of shareholder activism, based on power, legitimacy and urgency.

9 It appears that ESG concepts were first mentioned in the 2006 United Nations' Principles for Responsible Investment (PRI) report. This included the Freshfield Report and 'Who Cares Wins: Connecting Financial Markets to Changing World' published by the International Finance Corporation in 2004.

10 The study's findings do come with limitations. Because the data were hand collected, the sample size was relatively small which can limit the generalisabiltity of empirical findings. Another limitation relates to the use of *Vigeo Eiris* ESG ratings as the CSR perform-ance control variable. The *Vigeo Eiris* ESG ratings methodology is proprietary, and while the ratings seem to go beyond reliance on voluntary disclosure of companies, it is not clear how much of the rating is weighted on disclosure or other forms of independent

assessment of actual CSR performance. Finally, this study does not use multiple time frames, which could be useful for assessing the direction of the CSR–CFP relationship.

11 See also Jones and Frost (2017) for a study on the relationship between sustainability disclosure and the cost of capital across three international reporting jurisdictions: the United Kingdom, Hong Kong and Australia. This study also demonstrates that higher levels of sustainability disclosure are associated with lower cost of capital across reporting jurisdictions.

3

THE RISE OF SOCIAL IMPACT INVESTING

Introduction

In this chapter, we discuss the social impact investing (SII) concept in more detail and provide several definitions from a range of authoritative sources. We illustrate where SII is situated on the investment spectrum which ranges from traditional investments that seek competitive returns (and limited use of ESG factors) to pure philanthropic investments which can be described as 'impact only' investments. While many organisations and networks around the world have provided various definitions for impact investing, one of the more useful definitions is offered by the Global Impact Investing Network (GIIN). They define SII as

> investments made with the intention to generate positive, measurable social and environmental impact alongside a financial return. Impact investments can be made in both emerging and developed markets, and target a range of returns from below market to market rate, depending on investors' strategic goals.[1]

In this chapter, we stress that impact investing goes beyond corporate social responsibility (CSR) and environmental, social and governance (ESG) in two important ways. First, it aims to create a positive social impact, not merely avoid a negative impact. Second, it requires the measurement of social impact which is essential for assessing how much social value has been created from a social programme or intervention. In a sense, impact investing is very similar in principle to the creating shared value (CSV) concept where companies can potentially improve competitiveness and profitability by realigning their business models to address social problems and challenges. Both approaches seek financial returns alongside positive social impacts. Given the growing sense of enthusiasm and optimism for the potential of SII among global investors, we also consider the mismatch with the 'hype'

DOI: 10.4324/9781003225591-3

and the actual size of the global investment market and some of the key challenges facing the growth of the SII market.

Definition of Social Impact Investing

The Rockefeller Foundation (2012, p. vii) defined impact investing as involving: 'investors seeking to generate both financial return and social and/or environmental value – while at a minimum returning capital, and, in many cases, offering market rate returns or better'.[2] The GIIN (2020b, para. 1) defines impact investments as those which are

> made with the intention to generate positive, measurable social and environmental impact alongside a financial return. Impact investments can be made in both emerging and developed markets and target a range of returns from below market to market rate, depending on investors' strategic goals.

According to the GIIN, the characteristics of impact investing are as follows:

> *Intentionality.* An investor's intention to have a positive social or environmental impact through investments is essential to impact investing.
>
> *Investment with return expectations.* Impact investments are expected to generate a financial return on capital or, at minimum, a return of capital.
>
> *Range of return expectations and asset classes.* Impact investments target financial returns that range from below market (sometimes called concessionary) to risk-adjusted market rate and can be made across asset classes, including but not limited to cash equivalents, fixed income, venture capital and private equity.

Rodin and Brandenburg (2014, p. 7) similarly identify the most important distinguishing characteristics of impact investing as follows:

> At the heart of impact investing is the presence of dual objectives – the desire actively to achieve positive social or environmental results as well as financial ones.
>
>   Impact investing may complement philanthropy and be used by philanthropists, but it is not philanthropy – unlike grants, impact investments are made with an expectation of financial return.
>
>   Impact investing is more than 'doing no harm' – it is a positive investment made to an enterprise that has the potential to solve a specific problem or deliver a particular service while also turning a profit or at least becoming financially self-sustaining.
>
>   Both impact investors and the businesses in which they invest – we call them impact enterprises, although they are often referred to as social enterprises – track relevant financial as well as social and environmental performance metrics across their portfolios or enterprises.

Similarly, the G8 Taskforce on Social Impact Investment (2014) defined SII as investments 'that intentionally target specific social objectives along with a financial return and measure the achievement of both' (p. 1).[3]

It is clear from these collective definitions that impact investing goes beyond CSR and ESG in at least two important respects. First, SII aims to create a positive social impact or positive social outcomes, not merely avoiding a negative impact. Second, it requires the measurement of impact because the goal of impact investment is to contribute to social value creation. According to Cohen (2020, p. 64):

> ESG investments do not employ measurement but instead typically assess the effects of a company's policies in a qualitative and non-standardised way. Such assessment is inaccurate and makes it impossible to rely on dependable comparisons between businesses. In contrast, true impact investment removes the guesswork and replaces it with dependable market data.

The New South Wales Office of Social Impact Investment (2020b, para. 1)[4] expanded further on the definition of impact investing to include purpose and types of SII funding arrangements:

> This investment often brings together capital and expertise from the public, private and not-for-profit sectors to achieve a social objective. Investments can be made into companies, organisations or funds, whether they be not-for-profit or for-profit. Social impact investments can also be used to finance social services and social infrastructure. In these types of arrangements, payments are normally made based on achieving agreed social outcomes rather than on inputs or activities. Where investors are involved, they will usually expect their investment to be repaid and, potentially, to earn a return. This return is likely to depend on the level of social outcomes achieved.

Further, the Department of Treasury (2020, para. 1), in the context of its principles for SII, defines impact investing as:

> An emerging, outcomes-based approach that brings together governments, service providers, investors and communities to tackle a range of policy (social and environmental) issues. It provides governments with an alternative and innovative mechanism to address social and environmental issues while also leveraging government and private sector capital, building a stronger culture of robust evaluation and evidenced-based decision making, and creating a heightened focus on outcomes.

The investment spectrum

Figure 3.1 illustrates where SII is situated on an investment spectrum ranging from traditional investments with limited or no use of ESG factors to pure philanthropic

			Impact Investment		
Traditional	Responsible	Sustainable	Thematic	Impact-First	Philanthropy
Finance-only	Focus on ESG	Focus on ESG	Focus on issue areas	Focus on issue	Impact-only
Limited or no	risks ranging from	opportunities,	where social or	area where	Focus on issue
use of ESG	a wide	through	environmental need	social or	areas where
factors	consideration of	investment	creates a	environmental	social or
	ESG factors to	selection, portfolio	commercial growth	need requires	environmental
	negative	management and	opportunity for	some financial	need requires
	screening of	shareholder	market-rate or	trade-off	100% financial
	harmful products	advocacy	market-beating		trade-off
			returns		

| High-impact solutions |
| ESG opportunities |
| ESG risk management |
| Competitive returns |

FIGURE 3.1 The new paradigm

Source: Brandstetter and Lehner (2014, p. 89)

investments. Philanthropic investments can be described as 'impact only' investments, with the financial trade-off between social and/or environmental objectives being 100%. In other words, no financial returns are sought.

Next to traditional investing is socially responsible investing which focuses on ESG risk factors which can range from a wide consideration of ESG risk factors to negative screening of harmful products. As can be seen from Figure 3.1, this type of investment also seeks a competitive return. Sustainable investing also seeks competitive returns, but here the focus is the creation of ESG opportunities through investment selection, portfolio management and shareholder advocacy. Brandstetter and Lehner (2014, p. 13) note that 'integrating social and environmental factors into the process of investment analysis and proactively searching for sustainable companies is the main focus of sustainable investing'.

In Figure 3.1, 'thematic investments' extend beyond traditional, responsible and sustainable investing and focus on impact investments that actively deal with social and environmental concerns while still seeking a competitive return. This type of investment appears to be closest to the CSV concept discussed in Chapter 2. The CSV concept implies that the alignment between business priorities and social objectives need not be compromised by a financial-return trade-off. Conversely, 'impact-first' investors seek a financial return alongside social impact priorities but are willing to accept some financial trade-off in pursuing their social objectives. In other words, they do not seek a competitive return. It is acknowledged that Figure 3.1 is somewhat simplistic in its representation because definitions and investment strategies can clearly overlap.

Tagging social impact investments

An innovative approach to tagging different types of impact investments is proposed by Inter-American Development Bank (IDB) (see JP Morgan, 2015). The IDB identifies dimensions to the definition of impact investments which includes two key elements: business sectors and vulnerable populations. For an investment to qualify as impact investment, it must meet two basic criteria: (1) address either basic needs (e.g. agriculture, water, housing) or basic services (e.g. education, health, green energy and financial services); and (2) at least half of its beneficiaries must be vulnerable populations (see JP Morgan report, 2015, p. 12).

The IDB is currently in the process of developing a tagging methodology to classify investments as impact investments, based on four key filters:

1. Financial viability: A project must involve a financial instrument (private debt, guarantees or equity investment) and return at least nominal principal.
2. Development impact: An investment should generate social and environmental externalities, contribute to economic growth and/or private sector development and comply with ESG criteria.
3. Social impact: The investment should generate direct/visible social impact (see JP Morgan report, 2015, pp. 12–13).
4. Impact intention: The investment should follow a specific impact investing approach with a deliberate, measurable goal of generating social/environmental impact in addition to a financial return.

In the IDB framework, impact investments are differentiated from investments *with* impact. A social project is tagged as an 'impact investment' if it is structured using a financial instrument (debt, guarantees or equity); promises to return at least nominal capital; involves beneficiaries who are poor, low income or disadvantaged; and there is evidence of intention to provide social or environmental impact. This intention must be evidenced in the loan proposal and results matrix as well as a robust system to monitor impact. If the project involves a financial instrument and promises a return on nominal capital, is designed on a commercial basis and is likely to generate tangible positive impact but does not involve beneficiaries who are poor, low income or disadvantaged, then it is classified as an 'investment with impact' but with no specific intentionality (see JP Morgan report, 2015, p. 14).[5]

Defining social impact

Defining and measuring social impact itself is at heart of SII. Without an appropriate definition of social impact and a robust approach to measurement, impact investments cannot be properly evaluated from a risk–return–impact perspective (Saltuk, 2012; Cohen, 2020). The International Association for Impact Assessment (IAIA) defines 'impact' as 'the difference between what would happen with the action and what would happen without it' (n.d., p. 1). And further:

> The International Principles for Social Impact Assessment considers that social impacts include all the issues associated with a planned intervention (i.e. a project) that affect or concern people, whether directly or

indirectly. Specifically, a social impact is considered to be something that is experienced or felt in either a perceptual (cognitive) or a corporeal (bodily, physical) sense, at any level, for example at the level of an individual person, an economic unit (family/household), a social group (circle of friends), a workplace (a company or government agency), or by community/society generally. These different levels are affected in different ways by an impact or impact causing action. Because 'social impact' is conceived as being anything linked to a project that affects or concerns any impacted stakeholder group, almost anything can potentially be a social impact so long as it is valued by or important to a specific group of people. Environmental impacts, for example, can also be social impacts because people depend on the environment for their livelihoods and because people may have place attachment to the places where projects are being sited. Impacts on people's health and wellbeing are social impacts. The loss of cultural heritage, important habitats or biodiversity can also be social impacts because these are valued by people. SIA therefore should address everything that is relevant to people and how they live. This means that SIA cannot start with a checklist of potential impacts, but must identify the social impacts from an awareness of the project and an understanding of how the project will affect what is important to the project's stakeholders.

IAIA, 2015, p. 2

According to Vanclay (2003, p. 7), social impacts are changes to people's lives in one or more of the following areas:

- *way of life* – that is, how they live, work, play and interact with one another on a day-to-day basis;
- *their culture* – that is, their shared beliefs, customs, values and language or dialect;
- *their community* – its cohesion, stability, character, services and facilities;
- *their political systems* – the extent to which they are able to participate in decisions that affect their lives, the level of democratisation that is taking place, and the resources provided for this purpose;
- *their environment* – the quality of the air and water they use; the availability and quality of the food they eat; the level of hazard or risk, dust and noise they are exposed to; the adequacy of sanitation, their physical safety, and their access to and control over resources;
- *their health and wellbeing* – health is a state of complete physical, mental, social and spiritual wellbeing and not merely the absence of disease or infirmity;
- *their personal and property rights* – particularly whether they are economically affected, or experience personal disadvantage which may include a violation of their civil liberties; and
- *their fears and aspirations* – their perceptions about their safety, their fears about the future of their community, and their aspirations for their future and the future of their children

The IAIA (2015, p. 2) also draw an important distinction between a social change process and a social impact as the former does not imply the latter:

> Not all social change processes result in social impacts. For example, a modest increase in population is not necessarily a negative social impact as in many circumstances, it may be a benefit leading to economic growth and social development. On the other hand, an unplanned, rapid, large increase in population associated with a project (influx) can result in negative social impacts. The issue for social impact assessment (SIA) is how to best ensure that the process of in-migration is anticipated, prepared for, and managed adequately to minimise negative impacts and maximize potential benefits.

Explaining the emergence of SII

As discussed in Chapter 1, the emergence of SII can be explained in part by the changing view of free market capitalism following the global financial crisis (GFC) (2007–2009). As explained by Bugg-Levine and Goldstein (2009, p. 41):

> The economic crisis has shaken confidence in established investment ideologies and their mainstream proponents. The emergence of the impact-investing industry provides a potentially compelling alternative by offering to imbue investment with social purpose and, ultimately, to increase the scope of solutions to social problems that continue to proliferate even as philanthropy resources dwindle.

Bugg-Levine and Goldstein (2009, p. 41) see the wealth destruction and credit market contractions of the GFC era as having expedited the growth of the SII industry. The main drivers include high net wealth individuals and families seeking social impact but wanting financial returns as well; the ineffectiveness of traditional philanthropic options which are creating more opportunities for social entrepreneurs capable of innovating in the social impact space; a broader societal interest in addressing social and environmental challenges (the same social forces ushered in the CSR movement in the 1970s and 1980s discussed in Chapter 2); perception of social and environmental issues as important to business performance and sources of opportunity and growth (see Chapter 2). For instance, there is a growing recognition in the literature that better CSR practices are associated with more profitable firms (see Jones and Wright, 2018) and increased interest in private investment philosophies with public sector social delivery objectives. There is widely recognised that many pressing social challenges such as climate change cannot be addressed by governments or private markets alone. The impact-investing industry offers innovative solutions, such as social impact bonds (SIBs), which can bring private capital and government together to focus on specific social challenges.

According to the McKinsey Global Institute report (2020, p. ii):

> Public sentiment, as expressed in opinion polls over the past few years, suggests that we are living in a new era of rising discontent, mistrust of institutions, and an economy that does not work well for everyone. This remains true despite significant progress in some economic indicators, including employment rates and GDP growth, along with technological advancements and improvements in education and longevity.

Despite the growing prosperity of Western economies, persistent and intractable social problems continue. In the Australian context, the Australian Taskforce on Social Impact Investing report (2019, p. 8) reported some surprising statistics for a relatively affluent society such as Australia. For instance, around 12% of Australians cannot afford the basic essentials of life and around 3% of Australians have been living in income poverty continuously for at least the last four years. The Australian Taskforce reports that some of the groups who experience the highest rates of persistent disadvantage include Indigenous Australians, the unemployed, single-parent families and individuals with disabilities. The Australian Taskforce concludes (2019, p. 8): 'The challenges facing our society are set to become ever more complex – and it is unlikely that governments alone can find all the solutions'. According to the Australian Advisory Board on Impact Investing report 'Scaling Impact: Blueprint for Collective Action to Scale Impact Investment in and from Australia' written by Addis et al. (2018, p. 2):

> Despite progress in recent decades, no country is yet on track to meet the SDGs. Australia ranks 16th among G20 countries on SDG implementation and coordination mechanisms and ranked 37th in the 2018 SDG Index overall. Results for Australians living in circumstances of disadvantage have not improved in 3 decades and Australia ranks in the bottom wealthy nations on environmental policy.

A question remains why traditional philanthropy is no longer considered an effective tool in dealing with intractable social issues. As explained by Rodin and Brandenburg (2014, p. xii), while traditional philanthropy has been a powerful force for good, it operates on too small of a scale to be effective (see also UK Taskforce report, 2014).

> the funds contributed by global philanthropy, even when combined with the development or aid budgets of many national governments (themselves facing budget constraints), up to mere *billions*. The cost of solving problems such as water scarcity, climate change, and lack of access to health care, education, and affordable housing runs into the *trillions* of dollars [Emphasis in original].

Roth (2019) analysed the benefits of impact investment versus philanthropy using a robust modelling framework. He presents a mathematical model of social financing which delineates the role of impact investors relative to 'pure' philanthropists. He characterises the optimal scale and structure of a social enterprise when financed by grants and the optimal scale when financed by investments. Using a social enterprise (Husk Power) as a case study, his study yields two heuristics to guide impact investors. First, investments as opposed to philanthropy allow a financier to discipline inefficient spending. Second, investments may enable a social enterprise to exploit new opportunities for profit and may increase its scale relative to when it is grant financed.

Growth of the SII market

It is clear from earlier chapters that SII and related concepts have gained considerable traction and momentum in the academic, business and consulting worlds. But how much of this excitement has translated into hard impact investment around the world? Claiming to 'present the first rigorous analysis and estimate of the size of the impact investing market', the GIIN (2019) report states, rather optimistically, that 'since the term "impact investing" was formally coined in 2007, the industry has grown in leaps and bounds' (p. 11). The trend data may look strong, but the absolute amount of social investment compared to global traditional investment market still remains very small.

Relying on self-report data from many different sources, including family offices, foundations, banks and pension funds, the GIIN (2019, p. 6) estimated that over 1,340 organisations currently manage USD502 billion in impact investing assets worldwide (these are directly countable assets). The GIIN (2019, p. 6) report also estimated that over 800 asset managers account for about 50% of industry assets under management (AUM), while 31 development finance institutions (DFIs) manage just over a quarter of total industry assets. The majority of SII comes from developed markets, including the US and Canada (58%) and Western, Northern and Southern Europe (21%).

Overall, asset managers accounted for approximately 50% of estimated AUM, reflecting the fact that many impact investors choose to channel capital via specialised managers such as those investing in venture capital, private equity, fixed income, real assets and public equities. The GIIN (2019) report notes that although most impact investing organisations are relatively small, with about half managing less than USD29 million each, there are also many large players managing over USD1 billion each. It is concluded that:

> Overall, this research indicates that a significant amount of capital is at work to address the world's social and environmental challenges. And the market continues to grow rapidly, with new investors entering to establish impact investing practices and to allocate additional capital to positive impact.
>
> *GIIN, 2019, p. 3*

While aggregate AUM is estimated at USD502 billion, individual investor portfolios vary widely in size. Whereas the median investor AUM is USD29 million, the average is USD452 million, indicating that although most organisations are relatively small, several investors manage very large impact investing portfolios.

Size of the Australian SII market

Although the Australian government has shown keen interest in SII (discussed further below), the Australian SII market is still very small. The Oceania region (comprising mainly Australia in its survey) represents only 1% of the global SII investment market (see GIIN, 2019, p. 6). The Australian Taskforce on Social Impact Investing (2019, p. 2) notes that SII represents a broad spectrum of investments. The level of financial return also varies widely. Most SIIs in Australia range from AUD500,000 to AUD10 million – and several have provided returns of capital and modest annual interest payments (2.5%–8%). While there are isolated examples of larger scale investments (AUD10 million plus) the Australian Taskforce report (2019, p. 9) concluded:

> While there has been significant growth and development of the Australian SII market in the last decade and a number of successful case study examples, it is still at a relatively early stage. The Australian SII market is not unfairly described in some quarters as a 'cottage industry'.

The Australian Taskforce on Social Impact Investing interviewed several industry experts to gauge interest in the SII market in Australia. Based on this survey and interview data, the Australian Taskforce on Social Impact Investing report (2019, p. 24) identified three potential areas of SII growth which most appealed to stakeholders: (1) payment-by-results (PbR) programmes, including SIBs; (2) small- to medium-sized social enterprises; and (3) large-scale social enterprises and investments. It is noteworthy that the Australian Taskforce findings indicated there are only 13 SIBs and PbR contracts operating in Australia (as of 2019), ranging in investment size from AUD5 million to AUD14 million. The Taskforce noted that small- to medium-sized social enterprises (<AUD10 million turnover) are reasonably plentiful in Australia (about 20,000 social enterprises in total) but large-scale social enterprises (AUD10 million turnover or more) are less common. The Australian Taskforce was only able to identify six social enterprises in Australia with an annual turnover of greater than AUD50 million.

Addressing the mismatch of investor enthusiasm and actual social impact investment

While the global SII market has been growing rapidly over the past decade, the absolute size of the impact investment market is negligible in global terms. The outstanding value of global bond and equity markets was over USD200 trillion in 2020 so the SII market represents roughly 0.25% of this market (SIFMA, 2020).

Given the growing sense of enthusiasm and optimism for the potential of SII among global investors, including Australia, it is important to consider why there is something of a mismatch between the 'hype' and the actual size of the global investment market.

JP Morgan's (2015) impact investor survey addressed challenges to the growth of the impact investment industry in a detailed survey of investors. The survey was based on 146 investment managers, about half of whom were fund managers (57%). The rest of the sample comprised asset owners, with foundations representing 18% of the sample, diversified financial institutions/banks 7% and DFIs 5% (see p. 5).

According to the survey (p. 8), the top eight challenges to the growth of the impact investing market include (in order of importance): (1) lack of appropriate capital across the risk/return spectrum, (2) shortage of high quality investment opportunities with track record, (3) difficulty in exiting investments, (4) lack of a common way to talk about impact investing, (5) lack of innovative deal/fund structures to accommodate investors' or portfolio companies' needs, (6) lack of research and data on products and performance, (7) inadequate impact measurement practice and (8) lack of investment professionals with relevant skill sets.[6]

In the GIIN (2020a) impact investor survey, respondents were asked to indicate the greatest challenges facing the impact investing market over the next five years. Identified challenges included (a) 'impact washing' (when a business wrongly claims to participate in socially positive activities) (66%), (b) 'inability to demonstrate impact results' (35%) and (c) 'inability to compare impact results with peers' (34%). According to the GIIN (2020a) report, these findings highlight a need to advance impact measurement practices through the collection of transparent and comparable data (p. xviii). Interestingly, fewer respondents identified 'inability to demonstrate financial performance' (23%) and 'fragmentation of impact measurement and management approaches' (20%) as among the most significant challenges facing the market over the next five years.

There is quite limited academic literature exploring why the SII market has attracted relatively little institutional investor support. However, an empirical study by Del Giudice and Migliavacca (2019) examined factors influencing institutional investment participation in SIBs. The authors examined 67 SIBs across the world which were initiated since 2017. Using a regression framework to investigate the financial and contractual characteristics of SIBs, the authors documented that institutional investor participation is not primarily driven by financial returns but rather risk and contractual factors. For instance, their regression results showed that debt or equity funding is preferred over donations, and debt funding is more strongly associated with institutional investor participation in SIBs than equity funding. Contractual characteristics also seemed to play a significant role in explaining institutional investors' participation in SIB arrangement. Del Giudice and Migliavacca (2019) concluded that institutional investors are more likely to participate in an SIB where the number of participants is smaller and where a special purpose vehicle is used, as these factors can mitigate risks associated with agency and information asymmetry (see Del Giudice and Migliavacca, 2019, p. 65). Ormiston's et al. (2015) also provided some empirical evidence on investor attitudes to impact investing. Their study was based on 'over 50 instances of participant observation within the developing impact investment ecosystem' (p. 356). Ormiston et al. (2015, pp. 356–357) critically evaluated institutional investor concerns with impact investing (whether real or perceived) around five themes: (1) permissibility under statutory and general law duties. Ormiston's et al. (2015) observed that institutional investors in particular have been quite pessimistic about impact investing because of statutory constraints on their investment mandates; (2) uncertainty as to where impact investment is included within modern investment portfolios (for instance, should impact investing be considered as an emerging assess class or as an investment approach that can carried out across all established asset classes); (3) relative immaturity of supporting infrastructure typically used by investors for the origination, analysis and portfolio management of investments (for instance, lack of investment intermediaries to facilitate impact investments and a lack of a common approach to social impact measurement); (4) frustration with a narrow set of appropriately designed investment opportunities (such as limited scale, liquidity and diversification for impact investment opportunities); and (5) limited human capital to design, implement and manage an impact investment strategy. While these issues present serious challenges for the development of the social impact investment market, Ormiston et al. (2015) also presented evidence on how impact investors are trying to overcome these issues.

Key points from Chapter 3

Many organisations and networks around the world have provided various definitions for impact investing. One of the more useful definitions is offered by the GIIN:

investments made with the intention to generate positive, measurable social and environmental impact alongside a financial return. Impact investments can be made in both emerging and developed markets, and target a range of returns from below market to market rate, depending on investors' strategic goals.

Impact investing involves at least three different elements: intentionality to create social impact, investment with return expectations and a range of return expectations and asset classes.

The concept of impact investing goes beyond CSR and ESG in two important ways. First, it aims to create a positive social impact, not just avoid a negative impact. Second, it requires the measurement of impact.

Many factors have driven the growth of the SII market including the impacts of the GFC, wealth concentration among the 'investment-oriented', limitations with traditional approaches (such as philanthropy) and growing societal interest in addressing social and environmental challenges among other factors.

While traditional philanthropy has been a powerful force for good, it operates on too small a scale to be effective in dealing with large-scale social and environmental challenges such as poverty, lack of adequate education and healthcare, homelessness, refugee crises and climate change. SII can harness the power of capital markets to address large-scale social and environmental issues.

While Australian governments have shown keen interest in SII, the Australian SII market remains very small. It is less than 1% of the global SII market which in itself is quite small – about 0.25% of the total outstanding value of equity and bond markets.

In terms of the future development of the SII market, the Australian Taskforce on Social Impact Investing report (2019) has identified three areas which appealed to stakeholders in their survey and interview data: (1) PbR programmes, including SIBs; (2) small- to medium-sized social enterprises; and (3) large-scale social enterprises and investments.

However, there are only 13 SIBs and PbR contracts in Australia, ranging in investment size from AUD5 million to AUD14 million.

Given the growing sense of enthusiasm and optimism for the potential of SII among global investors, including Australia, there is something of a mismatch with the 'hype' and the actual size of the global investment market.

JP Morgan (2015) addressed challenges to the growth of the impact invest industry including lack of appropriate capital across the risk/return spectrum, shortage of high quality investment opportunities with track record, difficulty in exiting investments, lack of a common way to talk about impact investing, lack of innovative deal/fund structures to accommodate investors' or portfolio companies' needs, lack of research and data on products and performance, inadequate impact measurement practice and lack of investment professionals with relevant skill sets.

Notes

1 This definition is provided on the GIINs website at https://thegiin.org/impact-investing/need-to-know (viewed 5 July 2021).
2 This definition is similar to the World Economic Forum definition (2013, p. 6) which described impact investing 'as an investment approach that intentionally seeks to create both financial return and positive social or environmental impact that is actively measured'.
3 Similarly, Canada's National Advisory Board to the Social Impact Investment Taskforce report 'Mobilizing Private Capital for Public Good: Priorities for Canada' (2014, p. 4) defined impact investment as embodying three key characteristics: (1) investor intention: investors seek to allocate capital (debt, equity or hybrid forms) to investments from which they expect to receive a financial return (ranging from return of principal to market rate returns) and a defined societal impact; (2) investee intention: business models for investees (whether they are for-profit or non-profit enterprises, funds or other financial vehicles) are intentionally constructed to seek financial and social value; and (3) impact measurement: investors and investees are able to demonstrate how these stated intentions translate into measurable social impact.

4 According to its website, the Office of Social Impact Investment (OSII) is a joint team of the NSW Department of Premier and Cabinet (DPC) and the NSW Treasury. The OSII was established as an initiative of the NSW government to work with its partners and facilitate growth in the SII market. The OSII oversees and leads the implementation of the NSW Social Impact Investment Policy, working closely with other government agencies and non-government stakeholders. Key elements of this work include developing new SII transactions and building capability and capacity among agencies and others to participate in SII (see www.osii.nsw.gov.au/about-us/about-us-2) (viewed 5 July 2021).

5 www.jpmorganmarkets.com.

6 The OECD (2019) report (pp. 103–104) also alluded to the many headwinds facing the SII market across regions, including difficult business environments which can hinder market development (particularly in developing countries), lack of intermediaries in most countries, a lack of access to capital for many social enterprises, lack of awareness about SII at the policy as well as the practitioner levels, lack of a common understanding of social impact investment, lack of standardised approaches to impact measurement and the fact that most social enterprises and investors in these enterprises do not disclose investment details or transaction data (social enterprises often lack the resources for a full dedicated investor's relations and/or public relations team).

4

EVALUATING ALTERNATIVE TYPES OF SOCIAL IMPACT INVESTMENTS

Introduction

This chapter considers several different types of social impact investing (SII) funding models that are becoming more widely used in practice including social impact bonds (SIBs) (called social benefit bonds or SBBs in Australia), development impact bonds (DIBs), outcome-focused grants and payment-by-results (PbR) contracts. We explain the concept of an SIB which is essentially a funding model that pays a financial return to investors based on the achievement of agreed-upon social outcomes. We also explain the strengths and limitations of SIBs. While SIBs are widely viewed as a promising financing innovation, the literature is divided over their current effectiveness and future potential. Chapter 4 also discusses cost measurement issues in an SIB arrangement. We argue that capturing direct cost savings for government is relatively straightforward. However, measuring the indirect cost savings associated with the intangible benefits of a social programme or intervention is much more challenging and complex. We suggest a stated preference experiment approach for quantifying and monetising intangible benefits. Finally, Chapter 4 provides four illustrations of SIB and DIB arrangements in practice, including the Peterborough prison's SIB, the Educate Girls' DIB, the New Parent and Infant Network's (Newpin) SBB and the Benevolent Society Resilient Families' SBB. Most other SIB arrangements which have been developed around the world are based on a similar funding structure. The four case studies presented highlight the underlying complexity of SIB arrangements and the critical importance of rigorous outcomes measurement and evaluation in determining the overall success of an SIB.

Social Impact Bonds

Social Impact Bonds (SIBs) (or Social Benefit Bonds in Australia) are among the first and best-known SII funding models.[1] The G8 Taskforce on Social Impact

DOI: 10.4324/9781003225591-4

Investment (2014, pp. 3–4) envisaged a prominent role for SIBs in growing the SII market. The Australian Taskforce on Social Impact Investing report (2019, p. 23) also anticipates an important role for SIBs for the future of the SII market.[2]

Originating in the UK with the Peterborough project (see case illustration below), SIBs are essentially a funding model which pays a financial return to investors based on the achievement of agreed social outcomes. Figure 4.1 outlines the structure of an SIB. In the case of a commercial SIB, private investors provide the upfront capital for the social programme or intervention to be funded. Investors could be a Community Reinvestment Act (CRA) investment (in the case of the US),[3] institutional investors or banks. Investments are usually made through intermediaries who can structure, coordinate and manage risk for market participants. Service providers deliver the social programme or intervention (such as helping the homeless or at-risk youth). Service providers could be a private company, a non-government organisation (NGO) or a not-for-profit (NFP) entity. The service provider is required to meet agreed outcomes which are measured and evaluated by independent evaluators (often consulting firms). Outcome payers such as the government only pay when the social outcomes have been demonstrably achieved. In this sense, the financial risk of the social programme intervention is effectively shifted from the government to private investors. If service delivery outcomes are

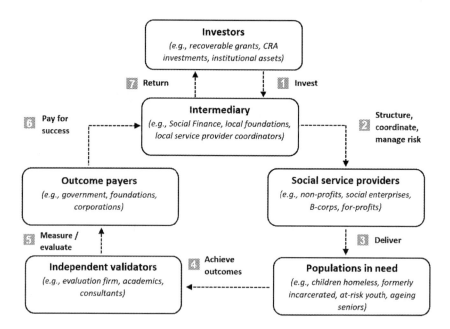

FIGURE 4.1 Structure of an SIB

Source: Organisation for Economic Co-operation and Development (OECD, 2019, p. 86). This OECD source also cited OECD report (2016) 'Understand Social Impact Bonds' where the image was adapted from Burand (2013)

not achieved, then investors do not receive their progress payments or return of principal. Outcome payments are determined from the cost savings to government from having the social programme funded by investors and delivered by service providers.

The savings generated by achieving social outcomes enable government to repay the upfront investment including a return to investors. Figure 4.2 shows how the savings can work for government. The status quo indicates what the full costs of the social programme would be to government with no SIB arrangement in place. This is contrasted with the savings to government with an SIB intervention in place. As can be seen from Figure 4.2, a successful SIB can reduce overall costs to government of social service delivery. Figure 4.2 shows three possible scenarios. The first is the status quo, which is the cost to the government if the government had to deliver the social programme. The second involves introducing an SIB arrangement. The SIB arrangement replaces the government in providing the social programme or intervention. The government will then make outcome payments on the event of the successful achievement of the agreed social outcomes. The potential cost savings retained by the government from the SIB arrangement is shown in scenario three (here the cost savings are the cost savings of the SIB intervention less the outcome payments (returns to investors and the cost of the intervention).

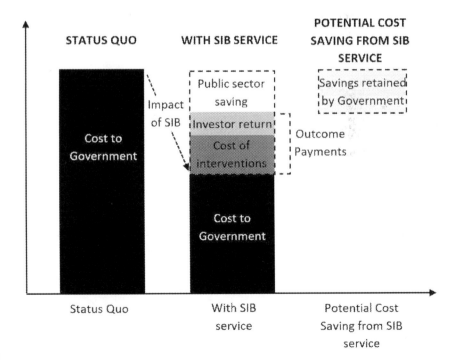

FIGURE 4.2 Cost savings from an SIB

Source: OSII (2018b, p. 31)

For a commercial SIB, private investors must be able to rigorously assess both the risks and returns of the social programme, determine the capacity of the service provider to successfully deliver the services and have the social outcomes measured and evaluated independently. Commercial SIBs involving private investors are likely to be more appropriate and have a better chance of attracting capital where the service provider has a successful track record in service delivery and the social programme being funded has a high prospect of success.

Other types of SIB

The Young Foundation (2011) identified other types of SIBs including (1) a philanthropic SIB, (2) a public sector SIB and (3) a hybrid SIB. With a philanthropic SIB, the investors in Figure 4.1 will simply be replaced by a philanthropic source of funding rather than an institutional investor or bank. One advantage of a philanthropic funder is that this type of investment may be less constrained by commercial risk factors, such as reliance on a service provider's proven track record, which may result in greater scope for experimentation and innovation in the delivery of a social programme.

With a public sector SIB, a government entity such as a local council could use internal funds or borrow funds to invest in a social programme, receiving a series of payments in the future from government where agreed social outcomes are achieved. With a hybrid SIB, funding could come from more than one sector, for example, from private investors and a charity. While this approach has the potential to unlock additional funding sources, it can also add considerable complexity and risk to the SIB in the sense that investors from different sectors may have different perspectives, objectives and motivations which must be managed for the SIB arrangement to succeed.

Outcome-focused grants

Outcome-focused grants are provided on the basis that results can be identified, achieved and measured. Grants may be offered by any public or private organisations. The grant could be on a one-off basis or organisations could be a co-contributor to a fund. The advantage of this approach is that it can provide social sector organisations opportunity to collect data and measure outcomes as well as providing data to the government and investors on what social programmes actually work in practice.

PbR contracts

To understand PbR contracts, we need to understand how the government-funding process works. Government procurement and contract management processes for social programmes are typically allocated via competitive tendering processes based on existing service delivery models and outputs. Government determines the policy and appropriate strategies to deliver on the social policy which is the basis for funding allocation to service providers. However, social outcomes are usually not rigorously measured, and there is no guarantee that any substantive social outcomes will ever be achieved. Nor is there any guarantee that government contracts will adopt the best or most innovative strategy that works best in practice. It is possible that governments do not know what approach works best (particularly for complex social interventions), and there is built in inertia and inefficiency such as a tendency to fund social services based on what has been done previously.

Under a PbR contract, government pays a service provider to deliver a social programme based on the results achieved. The advantage of this approach is that the government can specify the outcomes required, and the service provider needs to demonstrate that the social outcome objectives have been met. An SIB can be considered a special type of PbR contract that enables service providers to access capital from investors to deliver services in advance of getting paid. If the service provider achieves the results specified in the contract, investors receive a return on their investment.

Incentive payments

Governments can also offer additional payments to service providers beyond the cost of delivering a service if 'stretch' targets are met. These incentive payments can be used in traditional, PbR and other outcome-based contracts. As with PbR contracts, the additional payments may be required to be reinvested in service delivery.

Development Impact Bonds

A Development Impact Bond (DIB) works in exactly the same way as an SIB but with one key difference. In an SIB arrangement, the outcome payer is typically the government. However, governments in many developing countries do not have the resources to fund social programmes. In a DIB arrangement, the outcome payer is typically a private donor or aid agency rather than government. The advantage for the donor or aid agency is that substantial risks are transferred to the investor, and payments are only based on outcomes achieved (an example of a DIB arrangement is provided below).

If we consider a specific SII structure such as an SIB, there are many potential benefits for private sector involvement in social service delivery. According to the Australian Government Principles for Social Impact Investing (2019, p. 1), SII can meet particular needs and provide alternative and innovative pathways to funding social programmes:

> Social impact investing is an emerging, outcomes-based approach that brings together governments, service providers, investors and communities to tackle a range of policy (social and environmental) issues. It provides governments

with an alternative and innovative mechanism to address social and environmental issues while also leveraging government and private sector capital, building a stronger culture of robust evaluation and evidenced-based decision making, and creating a heightened focus on outcomes. The Principles acknowledge that social impact investing can take many forms, including but not limited to, Payment by Results contracts, outcomes-focused grants, and debt and equity financing.

The OSII report (2015, p. 2) envisages SII as having the capacity to deliver:

1. *Better services and results.* Social impact investment provides an opportunity to identify and test new and innovative ways to address social challenges, with a focus on measurement and delivery of outcomes.
2. *Better partnerships between the government and non-government sectors.* Social impact investment is an opportunity for governments to play an enabling role by creating the conditions for the non-government sector to do what it does best.
3. *Better value for taxpayers.* A strong social impact investment market will provide better value for money for the people, by driving greater contestability and innovation in service delivery and paying for results delivered.

According to Liebman (2011, pp. 10–11), SIBs also have the potential to overcome several obstacles to innovation and create more efficient and effective social service delivery. First, government funding is not always well aligned with successful outcomes and performance. In an SIB arrangement, investors and service providers have stronger financial incentives to innovate and find more efficient and effective solutions to social problems because their financial returns are based on this success. Second, government funding of social programmes often results in suboptimal or ineffective social programmes to perpetuate because of a lack of appropriate performance measurement and evaluation. SIBs have a much strong focus on impact measurement and achievement of social outcomes which reduces the risk of poor funding decisions to ineffective programmes. There is also much more transparency over which social programmes are likely to work or fail. Third, getting new ideas off the ground can be a very slow process. With SIBs, scaling up of a social programme occurs simultaneously with the rigorous evaluation of its impacts, greatly accelerating the expansion of successful social programmes. Fourth, innovation itself is risky, and government bureaucrats can be very wary of failure. Under SIB funding, government only pays up if the service provider delivers on the agreed outcomes (see Figure 4.1). Because the risk of squandering taxpayer dollars is effectively transferred to private investors, government funders will be more willing to commit resources to innovative approaches that are promising but not yet proven. Fifth, preventive programmes often do not get funded out of government budgets that they help reduce. By aligning payments to the achievement of future outcomes, SIBs have the potential to break down budget silos that hinder investments in preventative social programmes. Finally, performance-based funding requires upfront investments and the ability to absorb risk. The SIB creates a market-based mechanism for raising the upfront capital needed to finance a social programme and for spreading the failure risks that are inherent in any innovative activity (see Liebman, 2011, pp. 10–11).

Challenges with SIB arrangements

While SIBs are an exciting funding innovation, it needs to be recognised that SII is not suitable in all circumstances – they work best where existing policy interventions and service delivery are not achieving the desired outcomes or there is no social programme or intervention in place at all. Despite the significant potential benefits of SIBs, there are also challenges that need to be addressed. One criticism is that SIBs can be an unnecessarily complex approach to funding social programmes (Fox and Morris, 2021). Since government's cost of capital is typically lower than that of capital markets, it could be argued that government should be providing the finance directly, not through private investors. In addition, some philanthropists are concerned that SIBs risk diverting charitable funds to make up for public spending, essentially locking philanthropic money into government agendas.

While the Australian Taskforce on Social Impact Investing report (2019, p. 23) see the great potential of SIBs, they are not to be viewed as a panacea for all social issues. Further, high transaction costs, complexity of contracts and the time required to set these transactions up can be major obstacles:

> Social impact bonds can be of particular value for trialling new service delivery models. They also transfer some of the risk inherent in innovation from taxpayers to third party investors. But at the same time, social impact bonds are no silver bullet and will not – and should not – be used to fund the delivery of all social services. A key challenge to confront is the high transaction costs of individual social impact bonds. The contracts tend to be complex and slow to set up. The Taskforce is investigating ways to reduce the complexity and expense of setting up social impact bonds.

SIBs are a pioneering development without the benefit of tried and tested approaches for success. They typically involve quite complex negotiations between investors, the government and service providers in relation to the scope of the intervention, the outcomes to be achieved and how these are to be measured and evaluated. Much depends on the track record and performance of the service provider. If the service provider fails to meet agreed milestones or if the programme fails altogether, investors lose their investment as government has no obligation to make progress payments in these circumstances.

These arrangements can be further complicated where there is more than one service provider or multiple investors in the SIB. There are also major technical challenges associated with establishing rigorous and unbiased metrics for measuring impact. Another challenge is the type, nature and level of evidence required to assess the ultimate effectiveness of a social programme or intervention.

The Bridges Impact+ report 'Choosing Social Impact Bonds: A Practitioner's Guide' (see Goodall, 2014, pp. 7–14) provides a practical overview of how SIBs are operating in practice and the particular obstacles facing SIB arrangements. We know that SIBs have significant potential to unlock better outcomes through focusing resources on outcomes, stimulating innovation, catalysing entrepreneurial solutions and linking financial returns to outcomes (Goodall, 2014, p. 6) (see also Burand, 2013; Cohen, 2020). However, the design and structuring of an SIB arrangement is ultimately the key to its success. Goodall (2014, pp. 7–25) identified a number of design issues that require a successful SIB which include, among other factors, ensuring payment metrics directly relate to intended outcome (for all parties to agree the social outcomes have been, they need to be objectively and practically measurable), clearly define target beneficiaries (SIBs require a very clearly defined target cohort for the intervention, reducing the opportunity to 'cherry pick' those who are easiest to help), identify the full cost to society of the social issue being addressed so that service providers can price the delivery and establish an effective way of measuring for what would have happened with the intervention (consider the counterfactual, would the social outcome have been achieved without the intervention?).

There is also a growing body of academic and professional literature on the operations of the SIB market (see, for example, Ramsden, 2016). Much of this literature is quite recent having been published over the past decade. In terms of the operations, performance, risk and future potential of SIBs as an innovative financing tool, the literature is fairly mixed. However, the empirical literature is hampered by lack of solid empirical data on the performance of SIBs. A useful review of the academic literature on SIBs is provided by Fraser et al. (2018, p. 5) who state:

> Opinion is divided with both enthusiasm and caution around the potential that SIBs may hold for financing complex social interventions and reallocating performance and financial risk from the public towards the private sector.

As discussed above, strong proponents of SIBs see the SIB arrangement as representing a futuristic solution to potential public sector inefficiency and inertia by introducing private sector entrepreneurship and innovation and bringing together the usually separate private financial and social services sectors to solve difficult social problems (Cohen, 2020). However, Fraser et al. (2018, p. 5) state that:

> For others, it represents the worst of both sectors, involving the 'financialization' (a process whereby both macro-economic and public policy-making are subordinated to financial sector interests) of the public sector ... and perverse incentivization of the philanthropic and non-profit sectors to pursue commercial interests over their social missions ... as well as the risk that the

public sector will encourage commercial investors to make social investments by offering excessively generous terms. Moreover, it is possible that the subcontracted service will be suboptimal compared to a publicly provided service.

Fraser et al. (2018) reviewed 38 academic papers on SIBs and 63 'grey' sources such as consulting, government and 'think tank' sources. They identified three main themes from this literature review: (1) the role of public versus private values, (2) the importance of outcomes contracting and (3) the problematic nature of calculating and allocating risk for SIB projects. Three distinct narratives were identified: (1) a public sector reform narrative (the notion that public sector service providers have a number of serious limitations and shortcomings when dealing with entrenched social problems), (2) private financial sector reform narrative (for instance, social entrepreneurs who seek to achieve social impact as well as generating financial returns) and (3) a cautionary narrative (which is a more critical view of SIBs on pragmatic and ideological grounds) (Fraser et al., 2018, p. 10)[4].

Some major conclusions from the literature review are as follows: (1) there is a paucity of empirical evidence about the operations of SIBs in practice and most of the material reviewed is more in the form of opinion and commentary; (2) there is very little quantitative evaluation of impacts versus the status quo, and most operational SIBs are in the early stages of implementation; (3) the small number of predominantly qualitative empirical studies of SIB projects focuses on difficulties in establishing SIBs and determining measurable outcomes; and (4) the cautionary narrative is currently closest to the limited evidence available since it identifies the new challenges created by SIBs. However, the Fraser et al.'s (2018) study acknowledges that significantly more empirical research is needed to evaluate the strengths and limitations of SIBs including the merits of alternative funding models.[5]

Cost measurement issues for SIBs

While SIBs are a promising financing method for growing the SII market, government needs relevant and reliable information to make informed decisions about whether to enter into an SIB arrangement with market participants such as investors and service providers. For instance, government needs to know the full extent of its cost savings and whether these can be measured reliably (see Figure 4.2). The extent of savings will ultimately determine the return that can be paid to the investor. The better the return that investors can earn from an SIB, the more attractive the SII market will become as a source of capital.

While capturing direct cost savings for government is relatively straightforward, measuring the indirect savings associated with the intangible benefits of a social programme is much more challenging and complex. For example, a social programme which provides full-time employment to young offenders can be associated with direct cost savings (for instance, reduced dependence on unemployment benefits and higher tax revenues from employment status). However, a social programme which links up young offenders with employment opportunities may have numerous indirect or intangible benefits such as reducing crime rates, lowering health-care costs, reducing social problems such as domestic violence and family breakdown.

Generally, government disregards the indirect cost savings associated with intangible benefits and just focuses on direct cost savings. However, failing to capture the full cost savings, or at least make a reasonable approximation of these savings, can lead to inefficient resource allocation in the SII market. For instance, social programmes with higher overall cost savings to government (and higher social impact) may be more attractive to investors who can reap higher returns on their investment, and government, which reaps the benefit of more impactful social interventions.

A wide range of methods employed in the fields of economics and related literatures can potentially be used for pricing the indirect cost savings of intangible benefits from social programmes including (a) contingent valuation, (b) revealed preference experiments, (c) hedonic methods (a quantitative regression approach) and (d) shadow pricing among others. These methods usually involve the implementation of experimental surveys and revealed preference experiments, and where appropriate, accessing large datasets where quantitative modelling is involved. While these techniques can be time intensive and complex, they provide a more comprehensive basis for analysing and quantifying the full extent of cost savings to government on social programmes.

One approach to evaluating intangible benefits of a social programme is to implement an experimental analysis where respondents are asked to rank different intangible benefits or consider what they would be prepared to pay (say in additional taxes) for different intangible benefits. Consider a social programme that aims to reduce recidivism rates among young offenders in the community. A number of direct cost savings can readily be calculated including the direct cost savings for correctional services, policing costs and court services.

However, there are number of potential indirect benefits of the programme that can have significant positive outcomes for the community including:[6]

- Reduced pressure on health services
- More efficient and effective police force
- Reduced need for prisons and justice infrastructure
- Reduced physical damage costs to individual victims of crime
- Lower emotional pain and suffering costs to individual victims of crime
- Reduced costs to businesses (such as legal costs) due to criminal activities
- Reduced levels of lost productivity associated with the victims of crime (i.e. time spent in hospitals, fixing damage, absence from work, etc.)
- Safer communities because of less crime and anti-social behaviour.

While it may not be realistic or practicable to include all possible indirect benefits in the costing analysis, one approach is to design an experiment where respondents evaluate which intangible benefits they consider to have the greatest overall social benefit or utility. Using an experimental design, we could identify, for example, the top three intangible benefits of a recidivism programme and then attempt a costing of those particular benefits. Below is an illustration of how a simple orthogonal experiment can be designed where respondents are asked to rate their preferences for different combinations of alternatives (representing the intangible benefits) in terms of their overall social benefit. For the purposes of this illustration, the dependent variable is a binary outcome, where 1 = highest overall social benefit and 0 = lowest overall social benefit.

Figure 4.3 shows a randomised experimental design based on eight intangible benefits associated with the recidivism programme identified above.[7] For simplicity, each intangible benefit is labelled with only two levels (i.e. increased vs reduced and higher vs lower). In practice, the experiment could be made more complex by adding more levels to the intangible benefits and using a multi-class response

Profile Number 1

Card ID	Health_Service Impacts	Police_Force_ Impacts	Prison_Justice Impacts	PhysicalCost_Crime_Impacts	EmotionalCost_Crime_Impacts	Community_ Impacts	Business_Impacts	Productivity_ Impacts
1	Reduced_health_costs	Less_efficient_police	Increased_costs_prisons	Reduced_physical_costs	Higher_emotional_costs	Less_safe_communities	Increased_businesses_costs	Reduced_productivity

Profile Number 2

Card ID	Health_Service Impacts	Police_Force_ Impacts	Prison_Justice Impacts	PhysicalCost_Crime_Impacts	EmotionalCost_Crime_Impacts	Community_ Impacts	Business_Impacts	Productivity_ Impacts
2	Increased_health_costs	Less_efficient_police	Increased_costs_prisons	Reduced_physical_costs	Lower_emotional_costs	Safer_communities	Increased_businesses_costs	Reduced_productivity

Profile Number 3

Card ID	Health_Service Impacts	Police_Force_ Impacts	Prison_Justice Impacts	PhysicalCost_Crime_Impacts	EmotionalCost_Crime_Impacts	Community_ Impacts	Business_Impacts	Productivity_ Impacts
3	Increased_health_costs	Less_efficient_police	Reduced_costs_prisons	Increased_physical_costs	Higher_emotional_costs	Safer_communities	Reduced_businesses_costs	Reduced_productivity

Profile Number 4

Card ID	Health_Service Impacts	Police_Force_ Impacts	Prison_Justice Impacts	PhysicalCost_Crime_Impacts	EmotionalCost_Crime_Impacts	Community_ Impacts	Business_Impacts	Productivity_ Impacts
4	Increased_health_costs	More_efficient_police	Increased_costs_prisons	Reduced_physical_costs	Higher_emotional_costs	Less_safe_communities	Increased_businesses_costs	Increased_productivity

Profile Number 5

Card ID	Health_Service Impacts	Police_Force_ Impacts	Prison_Justice Impacts	PhysicalCost_Crime_Impacts	EmotionalCost_Crime_Impacts	Community_ Impacts	Business_Impacts	Productivity_ Impacts
5	Increased_health_costs	More_efficient_police	Reduced_costs_prisons	Increased_physical_costs	Higher_emotional_costs	Less_safe_communities	Increased_businesses_costs	Reduced_productivity

Profile Number 6

Card ID	Health_Service Impacts	Police_Force_ Impacts	Prison_Justice Impacts	PhysicalCost_Crime_Impacts	EmotionalCost_Crime_Impacts	Community_ Impacts	Business_Impacts	Productivity_ Impacts
6	Increased_health_costs	More_efficient_police	Increased_costs_prisons	Increased_physical_costs	Lower_emotional_costs	Safer_communities	Increased_businesses_costs	Increased_productivity

Profile Number 7

Card ID	Health_Service Impacts	Police_Force_ Impacts	Prison_Justice Impacts	PhysicalCost_Crime_Impacts	EmotionalCost_Crime_Impacts	Community_ Impacts	Business_Impacts	Productivity_ Impacts
7	Reduced_health_costs	More_efficient_police	Increased_costs_prisons	Increased_physical_costs	Lower_emotional_costs	Less_safe_communities	Reduced_businesses_costs	Reduced_productivity

FIGURE 4.3 Experimental design of intangible benefit preferences for a recidivism programme

Profile Number 8

Card ID	Health_Service Impacts	Police_Force_ Impacts	Prison_Justice Impacts	PhysicalCost_Crime Impacts	EmotionalCost_Crime Impacts	Community_ Impacts	Business_Impacts	Productivity_ Impacts
8	Reduced_health_costs	More_efficient_police	Reduced_costs_prisons	Reduced_physical_costs	Higher_emotional_costs	Safer_communities	Increased_businesses_costs	Increased_productivity

Profile Number 9

Card ID	Health_Service Impacts	Police_Force_ Impacts	Prison_Justice Impacts	PhysicalCost_Crime Impacts	EmotionalCost_Crime Impacts	Community_ Impacts	Business_Impacts	Productivity_ Impacts
9	Reduced_health_costs	Less_efficient_police	Reduced_costs_prisons	Increased_physical_costs	Lower_emotional_costs	Less_safe_communities	Increased_businesses_costs	Increased_productivity

Profile Number 10

Card ID	Health_Service Impacts	Police_Force_ Impacts	Prison_Justice Impacts	PhysicalCost_Crime Impacts	EmotionalCost_Cri me_Impacts	Community_ Impacts	Business_Impacts	Productivity_ Impacts
10	Reduced_health_costs	More_efficient_police	Reduced_costs_prisons	Reduced_physical_costs	Lower_emotional_costs	Safer_communities	Reduced_businesses_costs	Reduced_productivity

Profile Number 11

Card ID	Health_Service Impacts	Police_Force_ Impacts	Prison_Justice Impacts	PhysicalCost_Crime Impacts	EmotionalCost_Cri me_Impacts	Community_ Impacts	Business_Impacts	Productivity_ Impacts
11	Increased_health_costs	Less_efficient_police	Reduced_costs_prisons	Reduced_physical_costs	Lower_emotional_costs	Less_safe_communities	Reduced_businesses_costs	Increased_productivity

Profile Number 12

Card ID	Health_Service Impacts	Police_Force_ Impacts	Prison_Justice Impacts	PhysicalCost_Crime Impacts	EmotionalCost_Cri me_Impacts	Community_ Impacts	Business_Impacts	Productivity_ Impacts
12	Reduced_health_costs	Less_efficient_police	Increased_costs_prisons	Increased_physical_costs	Higher_emotional_costs	Safer_communities	Reduced_businesses_costs	Increased_productivity

FIGURE 4.3 Cont.

variable (i.e. more than two response outcomes). For the purposes of this simple illustration, hypothetical respondents were required to rate each card/profile in terms of whether it increases or reduces overall social benefit. Based on a sample of 32 hypothetical respondents, we use a logistic regression model to determine which intangible benefits were statistically significant and which intangibles exerted the strongest influence on the response variable. One of the most widely used behavioural models in the social sciences is the logistic regression model, which is set out as follows:

$$Ln\left(\frac{p}{1-p}\right) = \beta_0 + \beta_1 X_1 + \beta_2 X_2 + \beta_k X_k,$$

where $X_1, X_2, X_3, \ldots X_N$ relate to covariates (intangible benefits) measurement in the survey experiment and $\beta_1, \beta_2, \beta_3, \ldots \beta_k$ are the logistic regression parameters or weights of the intangible benefit variables fitted by the logistic regression model.

Table 4.1 shows the following results for the logistic regression model using hypothetical data.

This illustration model in Table 4.1 shows that most of the intangible benefits associated with the recidivism programme have a statistically significant positive relationship with the dependent variable. However, the three strongest statistical impacts (based on the Wald statistic) are 'health service benefits', 'safer communities'

TABLE 4.1 Logistic regression model for intangible benefits

	B	Standard Error	Wald	Sig.	Exp
Health service benefits	0.876	0.237	13.618	0.000	2.402
More efficient police	0.697	0.242	8.276	0.004	0.498
Reduced need for prisons/	0.522	0.244	4.592	0.032	1.686
justice	0.411	0.240	2.924	0.087	1.508
Infrastructure	0.232	0.242	0.913	0.339	1.261
Reduce business impacts	0.975	0.243	16.133	0.000	0.377
Reduced emotional cost	1.187	0.237	24.961	0.000	3.276
of crime	−0.481	0.243	3.923	0.048	0.618
Safer communities	−2.152	0.999	4.645	0.031	0.116
Reduced physical cost of crime					
Productivity gains from reduced crime					
Rates					
Constant					

and 'reduced physical cost of crime impacts'. If these are the most important intangible benefits associated with a reduction in recidivism identified by respondents, they may be candidates to be included in the intangible cost analysis. Similar experimental techniques can then be used to determine a 'costing' for the intangible benefits as rated by respondents. For instance, an experiment can be designed to investigate how much respondents would be prepared to invest above the base line direct cost of the intervention for any identified intangible benefits. This is one cost-effective approach to providing some measure of quantitative evidence in the costing of intangible benefits.

SIBs in practice: some case illustrations

Here we discuss illustrations of how SIB and DIB arrangements work in practice. For illustration purposes, we have selected: (1) the UK Peterborough prison project, the first SIB in the world; (2) the Educate Girls project, the first DIB addressing education issues, and the first used in Asia; and (3) the Newpin's SBB, the first SBB arrangement in Australia; and (4) the Benevolent Society Resilient Families' SBB.

Peterborough prison's SIB

The focus of the Peterborough prison's SIB was on short-sentence prisoners who exhibited high reoffending rates once released from prison. Sir Ronald Cohen (2020, pp. 23–24) was one of original instigators of the Peterborough SIB. He provides some insightful background to the project as follows:

> We met with officials from the British government and reached a deal: we would raise 5 million (pounds) ($6.7 million) to finance charitable service

providers that had been working with prisoners at the Peterborough jail. If, after five to seven years, we had failed to reduce the reoffending rate by 7.5 percent relative to the control group of released prisoners, no money would return to investors. However, if the rate of reoffending fell by 7.5 per cent or more, the government would repay the initial investment, in addition to a rate of interest that would rise according to the reduction achieved. The crux of this initiative was that the government would be paying out only 30–50 per cent of the money that would be saved on law courts and prisons: after paying back the investors, they still will come under budget.

According to Social Finance (2020), which was the intermediary which managed the Peterborough SIB, around 60% of short-sentence prisoners were convicted of at least one offence in the year after release. Each prisoner who reoffended after release in 2007 was convicted, on average, of five further offences within the year. However, these prisoners once released were on the fringe of society as no organisation or government agency assumed any responsibility for them post-release. Once released, they only had an average of USD61 to live on, 40% had no idea where they would be sleeping next, 25% faced challenges with addiction and 39% did not have enough money to make it to their first unemployment benefit or first job (Cohen, 2020, p. 123).

The SIB arrangement centred on an intervention called 'One Service' which operated at Peterborough prison between 2015 and 2017. This service provided 'through-the-gate' and post-release support for adult male offenders released from the prison and who had served sentences of less than 12 months. The aim of the intervention was straightforward: to reduce reoffending rates among this group of offenders. One Service contacted offenders before their release to introduce them to case workers who assessed their needs and planned reintegration activities. One Service worked with offenders for up to 12 months following their release. While the pilot was originally planned to continue until 2017, it was discontinued early with the introduction of the UK government's 'Transforming Rehabilitation' project. This initiative divided the probation service into two services – the National Probation Service (NPS), and a set of private-sector Commercial Rehabilitation Companies (CRCs) which were responsible for released prisoners, including those discharged from the Peterborough prison. Under the Peterborough SIB, the Ministry of Justice, supported by the Big Lottery Fund, entered into an agreement to pay a return to investors if specific recidivism outcomes or targets were achieved. In addition to coordinating the Peterborough pilot, Social Finance also raised investment funding from several individuals, trusts and foundations. Social Finance then used this funding to recruit a number of service providers (working under the One Service umbrella) to deliver a voluntary, through-the-gate service which included accommodation, help arranging benefits or addressing substance abuse and mental health issues. A number of service providers worked together to address key support needs including accommodation, training and employment, mental health and well-being and support to strengthen family relationships.

The Peterborough SIB operated on a payment by outcomes basis for the first two pilot cohorts. According to the process evaluation report (Disley et al., 2015), two cohorts of approximately 1,000 men participated in the pilot and were eligible to receive support from the One Service for 12 months following their release, as follows:

- Offenders in Cohort 1 were recruited between September 2010 and June 2012. The support period for Cohort 1 members ended in June 2013.
- Offenders in Cohort 2 were recruited between July 2012 and June 2014. The support period for Cohort 2 members ended in June 2015.

To be eligible to participate in the pilot, men had to be: (a) at least 18 years of age at the time of sentencing, (b) sentenced for a consecutive period of fewer than 12 months and (c) discharged from HMP Peterborough during the pilot after serving their sentence.

Under the SIB arrangement, the outcome measurement determined whether a payment was made to investors. An outcome payment (a return on investment) was paid by the Ministry of Justice and Big Lottery Fund for a reduction in the frequency of reconviction events of at least 10% in each of the cohorts, and/or a reduction of 7.5% for the cohorts who did not achieve the 10% reduction (Disley et al., 2015).

In July 2017, the Ministry of Justice announced that the Peterborough SIB had reduced reoffending of short-sentence offenders by 9% overall compared to a national control group. This exceeded its target of 7.5%. As a result, the 17 investors involved in the project received a single payment representing their initial capital plus an amount that represented a return of just over 3% per annum for the period of investment (see Cohen, 2020, for more discussion).

Educate Girls' DIB

The Educate Girls' DIB was launched in 2015 and concluded in July 2018. The goal was to improve education outcomes for primary school students in rural Rajasthan, Northern India, by funding the social programmes of 'Educate Girls'. Established in 2007, Educate Girls is an NFP that focuses on mobilising communities for girls' education in India's rural and educationally deprived areas. The project also provided an opportunity to test the viability of the DIB approach and explore 'whether the proposed benefits outweigh the costs of setting up and maintaining this complex partnership' (IDinsight, 2018 report, p. 5).

The investor for this DIB was UPS Optimus Foundation, a grant-making organisation that aims to achieve measurable long-term benefits for the world's most vulnerable children. Working capital was provided to Educate Girls, and social outcomes were independently evaluated by IDinsight, an NFP which partners with others to generate and employ rigorous evidence to improve social impact. The Educate Girls' DIB targets were to increase enrolment of marginalised girls and improve literacy and numeracy outcomes. Based on successful outcomes, the donor organisation, the Children's Investment Fund Foundation (CIFF), paid back the investor based on successful outcomes. Instiglio managed the project, designed the DIB and provided performance management support to Educate Girls.

As noted by the IDinsight evaluation report (2018), while improving public education is a priority in India, the state of Rajasthan presents particular challenges as 10% of girls aged 11–14 years are not enrolled at school. Less than a quarter of rural children in Grade 3 can read a Grade 2-level paragraph or solve a subtraction problem. Educate Girls sought to address these educational problems by encouraging families to send their children to school and by improving the quality of the education they received once they got there. Educate Girls provided training to community volunteers to make house visits and to deliver a child-friendly supplementary curriculum in classrooms to improve basic reading and mathematical skills.

Educate Girls' DIB had a project budget of USD270,000. The programme reached 7,300 children, covering 166 schools across 140 villages in Bhilwara, with an 80% focus on achieving learning gains and a 20% focus on achieving enrolment of girls (IDinsight, 2018).

IDinsight designed and conducted a three-year impact evaluation of the programme. They measured two outcomes to determine the final payment in the DIB: (1) learning gains of boys and girls in Grades 3–5 and (2) the enrolment of out-of-school girls. Learning gains, which accounted for 80% of the final DIB payment, were measured in a randomised control trial. The evaluation included a sample of around 12,000 students in Grades 3–5 across 332 schools in 282 villages. Half of these villages were randomly assigned to receive Educate Girls' programme, while the other half formed the control group.

According to IDinsight (2018, p. 6):

> IDinsight assessed students on basic literacy and math skills using the Annual Status of Education Report (ASER) testing tool. Student assessments were conducted at the beginning of the project (baseline) and the end of the three following school years; if students were not present at school on the day of the assessment, our surveyors assessed them at their homes. Learning gains were calculated as the difference between a child's learning level at baseline and at their final assessment. The impact was calculated as the sum of learning gains of children in treatment villages minus the sum of learning gains of children in control villages. Tying payments to this aggregate effect (instead of an average effect), ensured that Educate Girls would not face a penalty for successfully enrolling new students in school. If these students scored lower on assessments, their scores could bring down the average test scores in treatment villages. By adding their scores to the total instead, Educate Girls had a clear incentive to get even low-performing students into school.

The DIB was reported to have surpassed both of its target outcomes, with 160% of the final learning target achieved. In the final year, learning levels for students in programme schools grew 79% more than their peers in other schools – almost the difference of an entire additional year of instruction. Further, 116% of the final enrolment target was achieved with 768 eligible out-of-school girls identified in the programme area enrolled in school (against a target of 662).

In all cases, IDinsight reported significant differences in Year 3 of the programme and across all grade levels from Grade 3 to Grade 5. Average treatment effects, which denote the mean difference in learning gains between students in programme schools and students in control schools, were statistically significant at 95% confidence interval. UBS Optimus Foundation recouped its initial funding (USD270,000) plus a 15% internal rate of return. The total payout of USD144,085 was to be reinvested in UBS Optimus Foundation's grantee programmes, including a grant to Educate Girls (IDinsight, 2018, p. 9).

In terms of lessons learned, IDinsight stressed the importance of robust measurement and evaluation of social outcomes using control groups. Its evaluation report (2018, p.10) stated 'the benefits of DIBs' laser focus on outcomes can only be realized if those outcomes are measured correctly. Less rigorous methods, such as before and after studies, risk reaching the wrong conclusion about whether targets are met'. All parties involved in the DIB needed to be confident that they were being paid on the basis of actual social outcome performance and not extraneous or outside factors that may have affected the incomes measured.

Newpin's SBB

The New Parent and Infant Network (Newpin) is a therapeutic, centre-based programme that supports and empowers families to break the cycle of child abuse and neglect by providing safe, nurturing environments for their children (Social Ventures Australia [SVA], 2013). The focus of the Newpin's SBB was to either safely return children in care to their families or prevent them from entering care in the first place.

The NSW government initiated the Newpin's SBB, and UnitingCare was the service provider. SBB payments were linked to the expected long-term cost savings which would be shared with the investor group, SVA. SVA was the intermediary involved in the structuring and fundraising of the SBB. Investors subscribed to the Newpin's SBB and were entitled to share in the risks and rewards of the Trustee's sole material asset (the loan to UnitingCare). Key features of the Newpin's SBB are outlined in the Information Memorandum. The main financial and social outcome targets (SVA, 2013, pp. 3–8) include:

- At least 700 families will be supported by the Newpin project, of which approximately 55% will have at least one child under the age of five in out-of-home care.
- Over 400 children (across all centres) will be restored to parents.
- All family restorations are independently approved by the NSW Children's Court.

- Approximately $95 million in government savings over the long term, with around 50% to be retained by the Government and the balance directed to UnitingCare to fund the Newpin program and provide a return to Investors
- UnitingCare will receive approximately $50m under the Implementation Deed in the targeted scenario over the potential seven year life of the Newpin SBB. This will pay for the expected cost of the expanded program (approximately $41m over seven years) as well as the interest and ancillary costs of the Newpin SBB.
- Investor returns are based on the proportion of children participating in the Newpin program that are restored to their families. A variable Interest Rate is determined by the Restoration Rate outcome achieved. A Restoration Rate outcome of 65% over the full term would result in 12% p.a. interest
- The proportion of Principal repaid on maturity is determined by the Restoration Rate outcome achieved. A Restoration Rate outcome of 65% over the full term would result in 100% of Principal being repaid.
- Over the first three years, the Coupon Payments will be a minimum of 5% p.a and a maximum of 15% based on the restoration rate calculation.
- 100% of Principal will be repaid on maturity if the Restoration Rate is 55% or greater; and A minimum of 50% of Principal will be repaid in all cases.
- Early termination right for poor performance from Year 3 (if Restoration Rate falls below 45%)

The NSW Treasury commissioned a detailed evaluation of the Newpin intervention from the URBIS consulting group. Some of the key findings reported in the evaluation report (URBIS, 2018, p. iii) are as follows:

- Over four and a half years, the families attending Newpin have achieved a much higher rate of restoration than families in the Control Group, as well as a lower rate of reversal.
- Between 1 July 2013 and 31 December 2017, 53% of children in the Intervention Group (Newpin) were successfully restored to their families, compared to 18% of children in the Control Group.
- Newpin also has a lower rate of restoration reversal than the Control Group, with 13% of children attending Newpin who were restored to their families being subsequently removed into out of home care (OOHC), compared with 19% of the Control Group.
- The net restoration rate of 53% was significantly higher amongst the Intervention Group, compared to the 18% net restoration rate for the Control Group (p<.01). With 95% confidence, the net restoration rate for children in the Intervention Group is between 29.3% and 40.0% higher than the Control Group.

The Benevolent Society's SBB

The Benevolent Society's Resilient Families' SBB is a joint venture of the Benevolent Society, Westpac Institutional Bank and the Commonwealth Bank.

Over five years, the USD10 million SBB funded the Resilient Families Programme to deliver services to 303 families in NSW.

Under the SBB, private investors supported the pilot programme which is an intensive family preservation service designed to divert children from entering out-of-home care (OOHC) by improving family functioning and creating a safer environment for children.

The programme works with at-risk families for up to a nine-month period. There is an initial six-week intensive period where staff build trusting relationships and address immediate crises in a family. Together, staff and families deal with issues such as

- unstable housing
- debt problems
- regular income
- domestic violence
- substance misuse
- family functioning and relationships.[8]

Over the long term, staff and families work together so that changes will last and families are able to cope with future challenges and use other community services to help them. The Benevolent Society uses a Resilience Practice Framework which incorporates professional practices and approaches that have proven effectiveness.

In July 2018, the Benevolent Society bond became the first SII in Australia to reach maturity.[9] The five years showed positive results of families being supported to stay together, with 32% fewer children entering OOHC than children from a matched control group (i.e. those who received a 'business as usual' service). The programme also reported an 86% preservation rate of keeping children safe within their families.[10]

The results delivered capital-protected investors a 6% return on investment and capital exposed investors a 10.5% return. Returns to investors were calculated at the end of the bond (in December 2018), based on cumulative performance over the full term of the investment (all years). The programme is continuing as a PbR contract with the NSW government, with the current contract ending in 2021.

ARTD Consultants were engaged by the Office of Social Impact Investment (OSII) to evaluate the implementation and outcomes of the Resilient Families programme and to assess the appropriateness of the Benevolent Society's SIB measures. ARTD Consultants produced it final report for the Office of Social Impact Investment in 2020 (see ARTD Consultants, 2020). The evaluation was undertaken in two stages, using a theory-based, mixed-methods design with process, outcomes and economic assessments. The evaluation was carried in two stages:

> The process evaluation was the focus of Stage 1, examining the implementation and costs of the RF service and laying the groundwork for the outcomes evaluation; firstly, establishing the comparability of the Index and Control Cohorts, and then outlining ways in which outcomes would be measured.

In Stage 2 the focus of the evaluation shifted to outcomes measurement, while continuing to monitor key implementation factors including targeting; family engagement; and service focus, timeliness, duration and intensity. Stage 2 also included a case file review to better understand the DCJ business-as-usual service being provided to Control families.[11]

In their report, ARTD analysed data across the total measurement period (July 2013–2018) and drew on discussion and analysis from previous evaluation reports as well as: (1) NSW Department of Communities and Justice (DCJ) data for Index ($n = 303$) and Control ($n = 303$) Children – partial demographics, OOHC, Helpline reports, safety and risk assessments (SARAs) commenced and secondary assessments and historical child protection data; (2) Benevolent Society data for families who consented to their data being used in the evaluation ($n = 167$) – child and carer demographics, reported issues, service activity and outcomes data from the TBS Resilience Outcomes Tool; and (3) interviews with Primary Carers ($n = 17$).[12]

According to ARTD, a total 354 of families were referred to the programme during the SIB's measurement period. Due to exclusions defined within the SBB instrument, the population for measuring performance under the SBB consisted of a total of 303 Index Children and 303 matched Control Children. The evaluation drew on DCJ data for all of these children. Of the 354 families referred, 245 families agreed to participate in the programme and 167 consented to their TBS data being used for the evaluation.

Among the 167 families who agreed to receive the RF service and consented to their client service data being used for the evaluation, the average age of Index Children was 1.6 years old. Just over half (58%) were male, over one-third (36%) were from culturally and linguistically diverse backgrounds and almost one-fifth (19%) identified as Aboriginal and/or Torres Strait Islander. The average age of primary carers was 33 years, and almost all (93%) were female. Families' most common reported issues in referrals were child exposure to domestic and family violence (38%) and substance abuse by a carer (29%).

DCJ assessment data were available for all 303 families and showed the population included families with a range of risk profiles – 37% were assessed as low or moderate risk in their SARA completed prior to their measurement start date ('commencement SARA'), 45% were assessed as high risk and 17% as very high risk.[13]

In terms of performance outcomes, the ARTD evaluation concluded that the programme: (1) was effective in reducing the likelihood of OOHC placements, with 18 fewer Index Children compared to Control Children entering care during the measurement period. This difference was statistically significant ($p < 0.05$) and driven by a higher number of entries into care by the children in the Control Group in the first three months of the measurement period; (2) had the greatest impact in reducing OOHC entries for high-risk families, as seen through a range of risk lenses – commencement SARA risk level, carers' and siblings' OOHC history and families' prior SARAs – and in cases where the Index Child was unborn at the time of referral; (3) had a limited impact on the number of Helpline reports received for Index Children relative to Control Children; and (4) had a limited impact on the number of SARAs commenced for Index Children relative to Control Children. Similar to Helpline reports, Index and Control Children had an absolute reduction in the number of SARAs commenced over the measurement period.[14]

Key points from Chapter 4

Many different types of SII instruments are used in practice including SIBs (or SBBs in Australia), DIBs, outcome-focused grants, PbR contracts and incentive payments.

SIBs are among the first and best-known SII funding models, originating in the UK with the Peterborough prison project.

An SIB is essentially a funding model that pays a financial return to investors based on the achievement of agreed-upon social outcomes. Investors provide the upfront capital for the social programme which is delivered by a service provider – whether a private company, an NGO or an NFP entity. The savings generated by achieving social outcomes enables government to repay the upfront investment including a return to investors.

Other types of SIB arrangement include philanthropic, public sector and hybrid SIBs. They only differ as to who provides the capital. In a philanthropic SIB, a charitable foundation might be the capital provider (by way of example). Hybrid SIBs might involve a private investor and a charitable foundation as the capital providers.

Outcome-focused grants are provided on the basis that outcomes are identified, achieved and measured. Grants may be offered by public or private organisations as a one-off or organisations could be co-contributors to a fund.

Under a PbR contract, government pays a service provider to deliver a public service based on the results achieved. The service provider is responsible for covering the initial costs of delivering services. In this context, SIB is a special type of PbR contract that enables service providers to access capital from investors to deliver services in advance of getting paid.

Governments can also offer additional payments to service providers beyond the cost of delivering a service if 'stretch' targets are met. They can be used in traditional, PbR and other outcome-based contracts.

DIBs work in exactly the same way as SIBs but with one key difference. In an SIB arrangement, the outcome payer is typically government. However, governments in many developing countries do not have the resources to fund such an arrangement. In a DIB arrangement, the outcome payer is typically a private donor or aid agency rather than government.

There are many advantages to SII arrangements including better services and outcomes, better partnerships between the government and non-government sectors and better value for taxpayers.

SIBs are an innovated funding model that can potentially save public money by obtaining new sources of funding from the private sector and delivering social services in a more efficient and cost-effective way. SIBs can also achieve real risk transfer from the government to private investors. The focus on measuring and evaluating impact can lead to better overall social outcomes.

SIBs typically involve quite complex negotiations between investors, the government and service providers in relation to the scope of the intervention, the outcomes and how these are measured and evaluated.

In SIB arrangements, much depends on the track record and performance of the service provider. If the service provider fails to meet agreed milestones or if the programme fails altogether, investors lose their investment as government has no obligation to make progress payments under such circumstances.

Ultimately, the success of SIBs depends on how well the arrangement is designed and structured including (a) ensuring payment metrics directly relate to intended outcome; (b) clearly defining target beneficiaries; (c) identifying the full cost to society of the social issue being addressed so that service providers can price the delivery; (d) rigorously evaluating social impact; (e) ensuring all parties agree on whether outcomes have or have not been delivered, against which payments will be made.

There are also major technical challenges associated with establishing rigorous and unbiased metrics for measuring impact. Another challenge is the type, nature and level of evidence required to assess the ultimate effectiveness of a social programme or intervention.

The academic literature on SIBs is relatively recent with most academic and practitioner studies published in the past decade. While SIBs are widely viewed as a promising financing innovation, the literature is divided over their current effectiveness and future potential. However, given that SIBs are a relatively new phenomenon, there is insufficient empirical evidence available to provide a full assessment of their strengths, limitations and future potential. However, there are many examples of successful SIBs operating around the world.

While SIBs are a promising method for furthering SII, government needs relevant and reliable cost information to make informed decisions about whether to enter into an SIB arrangement with market participants (such as private investors and service providers).

While capturing direct cost savings for government is relatively straightforward, measuring the indirect cost savings associated with the intangible benefits of a social programme is much more challenging and complex.

Generally, government ignores the indirect cost savings associated with intangible benefits and just focuses on direct cost savings. However, failing to capture the full cost savings, or at least make a reasonable approximation of these savings, can lead to inefficient resource allocation in the SII market.

A wide range of methods employed in the fields of economics and related literatures can potentially be used for pricing the indirect cost savings of intangible benefits from social programmes including (a) contingent valuation, (b) revealed preference experiments, (c) hedonic methods and (d) shadow pricing among others.

Our suggested approach to evaluating the intangible benefits of a social programme is to implement an experimental design analysis where respondents are asked to identify *different intangible benefits. Using recidivism as an illustration, the experiment can identify the strongest and most statistically significant intangible benefits as rated by respondents. Further experimentation can identify the price respondents would be prepared to pay for these intangible benefits (this will allow intangible cost savings to be monetised).*

The Peterborough prison's SIB, Educate Girls' DIB, Newpin's SBB and the Benevolent Society Resilient Families' SBB were all a first of their kind. Most other SIBs which have been developed around the world are based on a similar funding and governance structure.

The four case studies presented highlight the underlying complexity of SIB arrangements and the critical importance of measuring and evaluating social outcomes in determining the overall success of social programmes.

Notes

1 However, as noted by Fraser et al. (2018, p. 5) and others, SIBs are not really bonds per se, as the financial returns are contingent on the success of the project being financed (more akin to equity than a debt instrument). Further, there is no evidence that SIBs can be actively traded once they are established; hence, there is no pricing for risk (see also Burand, 2013, p. 459, Fn36).

2 The Canadian Social Impact Investment Taskforce report (2014, p. 27) also indicated the importance of SIBs: 'One of the most visible examples of a government-enabled impact investment, SIBs have been issued in a number of countries including the UK, US, the Netherlands, Australia, and most recently, Canada'.

3 The Community Reinvestment Act (1977) is a US federal law designed to encourage commercial banks and savings associations to help with borrower needs across in all segments of the community, such as low-income areas.

4 For instance, McHugh et al. (2013) challenged the 'win-win' arguments of SIBs and calls for more research on their strengths and limitations including an evaluation of alternative funding approaches. The authors raise questions about the complexities of SIB funding arrangements and the inherent difficulties in measuring social outcomes. Tan et al. (2019) also questions the 'win-win' argument for governments and service providers. Tan et al. (2019) conclude that SIBs are 'strategically ambiguous' and policymakers should be cautious about using SIBs due to, inter alia, issues relating to their contractual complexity, accountability and transparency.

5 Hulse et al. (2021) examined SIBs in the more specialised context of financing health systems responses to non-communicable diseases (NCDs). Overall, they concluded that there is limited evidence on the effectiveness of SIBs which underscores the need for more 'high-quality studies, particularly economic evaluations and qualitative studies on the benefits to target populations, and greater transparency from the private sector, in order to ensure improved SIBs for preventing NCDs' (p. 1).

6 The OSII Technical Guide was used in this illustration (2018, pp. 34–35).

7 The randomised stated preference experiment was generated in the SPSS software package (Version 25).

8 www.osii.nsw.gov.au/initiatives/sii/the-benevolent-society-bond (viewed 5 July 2021).

9 www.benevolent.org.au/about-us/innovative-approaches/social-benefit-bond (viewed 5 July 2021).

10 www.benevolent.org.au/about-us/innovative-approaches/social-benefit-bond (viewed 5 July 2021).

11 See ARTD's 'Evaluation of the Resilient Families Service' www.osii.nsw.gov.au/assets/office-of-social-impact-investment/Evaluation-of-the-Resilient-Families-Service-Final-Evaluation-April-2020.pdf (pp. vii–viii) (viewed 5 July 2021).

12 See ARTD's 'Evaluation of the Resilient Families Service' www.osii.nsw.gov.au/assets/office-of-social-impact-investment/Evaluation-of-the-Resilient-Families-Service-Final-Evaluation-April-2020.pdf (pp. vii–viii) (viewed 5 July 2021).

13 The final evaluation report by ARTD Consultants (2020, pp. xii–xiii) made several recommendations to the NSW Department of Communities and Justice (DCJ) including that the DCJ should continue to invest in the Resilient Families programme as an option for families where children are at high risk of entering care.

14 See ARTD's 'Evaluation of the Resilient Families Service' www.osii.nsw.gov.au/assets/office-of-social-impact-investment/Evaluation-of-the-Resilient-Families-Service-Final-Evaluation-April-2020.pdf (pp. xi–xii) (viewed 20 June 2021).

5

INTERNATIONAL APPROACHES TO GROWING AND REGULATING THE SOCIAL IMPACT INVESTMENT MARKET

Introduction

This chapter considers various international approaches to growing and regulating the social impact investing (SII) market, with a particular focus on Taskforce findings and recommendations from the G8,[1] Canada and Australia. We also consider recommendations from the Global Steering Group for Impact Investment (GSG) and the Organisation for Economic Co-operation and Development (OECD).

In the Australian context, we consider a number of federal and state government initiatives to promote the SII market and contrast these with various international approaches. One important Australian initiative was the establishment of a Taskforce on Social Impact Investing by the Commonwealth government as part of the 2019–2020 budget. The role of this Taskforce is to examine the current state of play of social impact investing in Australia and provide set of strategies and policy recommendations to facilitate the growth of the SII market in this country. Many of the Australian Taskforce's findings and recommendations closely align with the recommendations of other international investigations, particularly the G8's Social Impact Investment Taskforce (2014), which was launched under the UK's presidency of the G8. We consider the specific recommendations of these reports including current SII initiatives at the state and federal levels in Australia.

The G8 Social Impact Investment Taskforce

The G8 Social Impact Investment Taskforce (G8 Taskforce) was an independent taskforce launched under the UK's presidency of the G8. The initiative was announced by the then Prime Minister David Cameron at the G8 Social Impact Investment Forum in June 2013. As stated by David Cameron at the World Economic Forum in Davos (Ahmed, 2013):

DOI: 10.4324/9781003225591-5

> I want to use our G8 presidency to push this agenda forward. We will work with other G8 nations to grow the social investment market and increase investment, allowing the best social innovations to spread and help tackle our shared social and economic challenges.[2]

The G8 Taskforce comprised government officials and leaders from finance, the business world and the charitable sectors across the G8 countries. Australia was also represented on the G8 Taskforce with observer status by Rosemary Addis, who established the Australian Advisory Board on Impact Investing (AAB) in 2013.[3] One of the important themes of the G8 Taskforce report is that SII is a rapidly growing market with vast unlocked potential to tackle entrenched social issues. The G8 Taskforce report (p. 3) envisaged a 'potential quickly to unleash up to $1 trillion of new investment to tackle social problems more innovatively and effectively'.

The rise of SII is also a response to a growing recognition that governments are more cash strapped than ever, and public sector service delivery can be both very costly and inefficient. The G8 Taskforce report (p. 1) stressed that the social problems facing 21st society are simply too mammoth and complex for governments and social enterprises working alone to solve. There is now a pressing need for more innovative and cost-effective funding solutions to solve difficult social challenges. The G8 Taskforce report also concluded:

> Old problems are proving more resistant than expected to efforts to solve them, whilst some problems such as diabetes and recidivism are taking on a new urgency and may well prove cheaper to prevent than the costs of dealing with their consequences.
>
> *p. 1*

Another major theme of the G8 Taskforce report is that the development of the SII market will only reach 'critical mass' and make a difference to the world if all market participants work together with a shared vision, including business interests, government, investors and social entrepreneurs. Tinkering at the edges of a worn out and inefficient system is not the solution – a much more radical and permanent reshaping of the capitalist system is required. In the words of Sir Ronald Cohen, the Chairman of the G8 Taskforce, social impact investing needs to harness the forces of 'entrepreneurship, innovation and capital' and use the 'invisible heart' of markets to guide the 'invisible hand' (Letter to Leaders of Taskforce Governments from Taskforce Chair, p. i).

The G8 Taskforce report (p. 6) provided a set of ambitious but clear recommendations. The recommendations focused on setting measurable impact objectives for the social sector and tracking their achievement, rethinking the traditional risk–return relationship to include the added dimension of social impact,[4] revamping the traditional fiduciary responsibilities of trustees to allow them to consider both social impact and financial returns on investments, streamlining payment-for-success commissioning, establishing an impact investment wholesaler to help grow the SII market, adopting strategies to boost social sector organisational capacity, providing profit-with-purpose businesses the ability to lock-in mission and supporting impact investment's role in international development.

The specific high-level recommendations of the Taskforce report are set out as follows (p. 6):

Recommendation 1: *Set measurable impact objectives and track their achievement.*

Recommendation 2: *Investors to consider three dimensions: risk, return and impact.*

Recommendation 3: *Clarify fiduciary responsibilities of trustees: to allow trustees to consider social as well as financial return on their investments.*

Recommendation 4: *Pay-for-success commissioning: governments should consider streamlining pay-for-success arrangements such as social impact bonds and adapting national ecosystems to support impact investment.*

Recommendation 5: *Consider setting up an impact investment wholesaler funded with unclaimed assets to drive development of the impact investment sector.*

Recommendation 6: *Boost social sector organisational capacity: governments and foundations to consider establishing capacity-building grants programmes.*

Recommendation 7: *Give Profit-with-Purpose businesses the ability to lock-in mission: governments to provide appropriate legal forms or provisions for entrepreneurs and investors who wish to secure social mission into the future.*

Recommendation 8: *Support impact investment's role in international development: governments to consider providing their development finance institutions with flexibility to increase impact investment efforts. Explore creation of an Impact Finance Facility to help attract early-stage capital, and a DIB Social Outcomes Fund to pay for successful development impact bonds.*[5]

For these recommendations to become a reality, the G8 Taskforce report (p. 43) also envisaged governments to have a vital role in stimulating the SII market in the following ways: (1) as a market builder, (2) as a purchaser of social outcomes and (3) as a market steward. The G8 Taskforce provided a number of specific recommendations in this regard (pp. 43–45):

1. *Government as a market builder.* As a market builder, government can provide resources and support to improve the viability and growth prospects of impact-driven organisations. Examples of how this can be achieved include capability-building grants and improving the access of social entrepreneurs to capital markets. Government can also act as a developer of an impact investment culture, with a range of intermediaries that manage impact capital and provide professional advice and services to the sector (p. 44).[6] Finally, government can encourage new investors to enter the SII market. Examples of how this can be achieved include providing tax and regulatory incentives for impact investment and examining initiatives to bring SII to the retail investor market.

2. *Government as a purchaser of social outcomes.* This can be achieved by initiatives such as broadening the use of outcome-based commissioning (where services

are provided on an outcomes rather than an output basis) and increasing the flow of investment from mainstream investors to impact-driven organisations.[7]

3. *Government as a market steward.* The G8 Taskforce report (p. 44) also recommended that government can provide an appropriate regulatory and legal framework to support impact-driven organisations. Examples of how this can be achieved include creating legal forms or regulations that protect the social mission of impact-driven businesses; relaxing regulations that prevent social sector organisations from generating revenues; and reducing legal and regulatory barriers for potential impact investors (G8 Taskforce report, p. 44).[8] Many of these recommendations are very similar to the Australian Taskforce on Social Impact Investing report recommendations (2019) discussed below.

Sir Ronald Cohen reiterated several of these recommendations in his recent book *Reshaping Capitalism to Drive Real Change* (2020) but provides some further insightful recommendations for growing the SII market. For instance, he recommends that government requires companies to measure social impact as well as collect and audit their impact activities (in a similar way that we have regulation governing the disclosure and audit of financial information provided by companies). The rigorous measurement and reporting of social impacts is critical to the success of the SII market as we discuss in Chapter 7. Cohen (2020, p. 161) also recommends that government publish data on the cost of social issues, such as the unit cost database published by the UK Cabinet Office in 2014. As discussed in Chapter 4, understanding the costs of social issues is clearly vital for quantifying cost savings and financial returns in a social impact bond arrangement.

Further recommendations by Cohen (2020, pp. 160–166) include appointing a cabinet-level minister to lead social impact policy to ensure that social impact investment is an active part of government policy; as well as incorporating social impact investment into international development aid. We discuss several of these recommendations later in this book.

The G8 Taskforce was superseded by the Global Social Impact Investment Steering Group (GSG) in August 2015. The GSG has continued the work of the G8 Taskforce with a wider membership, comprising 13 countries plus the European Union (EU), and active observers from government and leading network organisations supportive of impact investment. The Australian Advisory Board on Social Impact Investing was 1 of 23 such National Advisory Board (NAB) members of the GSG and one of the first established.

The GSG 2020 Impact Summit: *Leaders' Declaration for a Just and Sustainable Future*, addressed to G7 and G20 Leaders, Finance Ministers and Central Bank Governors, echoed many of the recommendations of the G8 Taskforce report. The Declaration emphasised the importance of situating social and environmental at the heart of the economy as well as stressing the importance of social impact-led recovery from COVID. The Declaration outlined three major themes: (1) the need to incentivise and scale up social impact investment; (2) mandating that companies provide audited disclosure of their social and environmental impacts; and (3) amending legislation and regulation to facilitate social impact investments by companies, pension funds and charitable endowments. The full Declaration is outlined as follows:

To save billions of people from hardship we must urgently put social and environmental impact at the heart of our economies

The Covid-19 Crisis has created an urgent need for a just, impact-led recovery that serves all people and preserves our planet. It presses us to change our ways, so that we can better address the great social and environmental challenges ahead of us. To save billions of people from greater hardship, it is urgent that we bring impact to the heart of our economies and put the following into action:

1. Scale impact investment to combat unemployment, reduce inequality and preserve the environment

Introduce incentives to accelerate impact investment, which seeks social as well as financial returns in order to create sustainable jobs, advance education, improve healthcare, and fund the expansion of non-profit organizations that support the most vulnerable.

Spur investment into small and medium-sized impact-driven businesses and high-growth impact ventures in developed and developing countries, to create millions of new jobs. Since many large companies are streamlining their operations and eliminating jobs, impact growth ventures and SMEs provide the best route to creating new jobs and supporting the recovery.

2. Mandate impact transparency for companies

Establish impact transparency by mandating that companies publish audited financial accounts that reflect their social and environmental impacts. This will provide ESG investors and consumers with the transparency they need to hold businesses accountable for the harm they cause and reward them for the positive impact they create.

3. Introduce legislation to empower companies and investors to pursue impact

Shift our economies away from profit alone to profit and impact. Amend legislation and regulations to allow companies, pension funds and charitable endowments to base their decisions on return and impact.

We are at an historic crossroad. Our future is in our hands. There has never been a greater need or a greater time to transform our economies so they better serve society and preserve our planet. We call on everyone – governments, citizens, consumers, investors, companies and philanthropists – to support implementation of these measures and pave the way to a fairer and more sustainable world.[9]

Canada's approach

Following in the footsteps of the G8 Taskforce, the National Advisory Board to the Social Impact Investment Taskforce (2014) was formed to focus on social impact investing issues in Canada. The Canadian Social Impact Investment Taskforce (Canadian Taskforce) report identified two priorities for social impact investing (p. 6): (1) addressing legislative and policy barriers to social entrepreneurship and impact investment in the non-profit and charitable sector, with a particular focus on the *Income Tax Act* and (2) encouraging impact investment through 'catalytic capital' measures (Canadian Taskforce report, p. 7).[10]

Many of these recommendations are similar to the G8 Taskforce recommendations. In terms of the first priority, the Canadian Taskforce report recommended (p. 7): (a) enabling charity and not-for-profit social enterprise activity by allowing charities and a subset of non-profit organisations (NPOs) with clear public benefit objectives to pursue certain related business activities on an income tax exempt basis and to pursue other business activities subject to income tax, and allowing charities to provide a private benefit where it is necessary to achieve a broader public benefit; and (b) unlock foundation capital for impact investing by clarifying that impact investments can be part of a balanced portfolio under current prudent investor rules (under provincial jurisdiction); altering trust law to state that, in the case of a charity, a prudent investor should consider social impact (under provincial jurisdiction); allowing charities to make below market rate investments where appropriate to advance their charitable objectives; and allowing charities to invest in limited partnerships.

A second major recommendation related to the government's role in stimulating investment opportunities (Canadian Taskforce report, p. 8). Specific recommendations include (a) establishing an impact investing matching programme, paired with appropriate incentives. According to the Taskforce report, this could

> take the form of a fund, capitalized by the government, which would co-invest with private investors, either directly in eligible social enterprises or projects, or in impact investment funds that require additional capital to close a funding round. Similar activities could be undertaken using a pool of grant money and request for proposals approach.
>
> *p. 8*

(b) establish an outcomes payment fund. According to the Taskforce report (p. 8):

> A dedicated fund for outcomes payments would catalyze the development of outcomes-based approaches to service delivery within and outside of governments. The government could specify maximum prices that it is willing to pay per outcome, as has been done in the United Kingdom, enabling the market to respond with innovative solutions.

Other supporting recommendations where government can provide a catalyst of the SII market include providing support for investment and contract readiness to develop the pipeline of investment opportunities, embedding initiatives into a broader strategy for building Canada's impact investment market and coordinating with all levels of government and engaging investors in the design of these initiatives (Canadian Taskforce report, p. 8).

Australia's approach

In terms of social impact trends, the OECD report (2019, p. 126) rated Australia as the most mature SII market in the region based on active local established intermediaries to facilitate social impact investing and the extent of existing government support. In terms of established intermediaries, there are entities such as Social Ventures Australia (SVA) which is actively seeking to grow the SII market in Australia in a variety of ways including establishing several social impact bonds (SIBs) (see Chapter 7).[11] Furthermore, there have been proposals in Australia to create a social investment wholesaler comparable to Big Society Capital in the UK (see Addis et al., 2015).[12]

Government interest in facilitating an active SII market has also been noticeable. Australian federal and state governments have taken a number of important steps to promote the Australian SII market. For instance, the McClure (2015) report recommended that government expand the use of outcome-based contracting which was also a key recommendation of the G8 Taskforce report (and several other government studies and reports). The 2017–2018 budget included funding for SII trials across the country. In 2017, the Commonwealth Treasury (Department of Treasury, 2020) established six high-level SII principles for guiding federal government activity and initiatives in the emerging SII market:[13]

1. *Government as market enabler and developer.* This principle stresses the importance of the government's role as an enabler of a new market and to address regulatory barriers that might impede the development of the SII market. Further, social impact investments made by government should be ready to 'leverage additional private capital or other investment opportunities to grow the social investment market in Australia'.[14]
2. *Value for money.* Social impact investments should only be contemplated where they offer a cost-effective way for government to deliver social outcomes and where the benefits exceed the cost of the investment.[15]
3. *Robust outcome-based measurement and evaluation.* Social impact investments should only proceed where there is clear agreement between investors and social delivery providers on the social outcomes to be delivered. Rigorous measurement and evaluation of outcomes is clearly critical to effective social impact investment. The Australian Government Principles of Social Impact Investing states: 'Ongoing outcomes-based measurement will be used to

monitor the progress, risk and returns of the investment, allowing for the investment to be refined as appropriate'.[16]

4. *Fair sharing of risk and return.* The Australian Government Principles of Social Impact Investing states: 'Opportunities to invest, and the risks and returns of those investments, should be fairly shared between parties to the investment'.[17]

5. *Outcomes that align with the Australian Government's policy priorities.* Social impact investments should be aligned with the current social and/or environmental priorities of government.[18]

6. *Co-design.* The Australian Government Principles of Social Impact Investing states:

> To encourage better outcomes in social service delivery and provide for innovation, social impact investments made by the Australian Government should be designed in collaboration with a broad range of stakeholders, including subject matter experts, and the communities and stakeholders who will implement them.[19]

There have also been a number of SII developments at the state and territory government levels. For instance, the Queensland State government has published a Social Enterprise Strategy (August 2019)[20] and developed a social enterprise grants programme.[21] The Victorian State government has also published a Social Enterprise Strategy in 2017 and recently announced support for a Victorian Social Enterprise Network.[22] In 2012, the Western Australian State government established a two-year pilot Social Investment Fund and more recently various data integration projects. In 2017, South Australian State government established a social impact bond focused on homelessness and is currently developing social impact initiatives in collaboration with the Commonwealth Government (see Australian Taskforce report, 2019, for initiatives in other states and territories). As discussed in Chapter 4, the state of New South Wales has a dedicated Office of Social Impact Investment (OSII) which is committed to delivering two social impact investments per year. The OSII is a joint team of the NSW Department of Premier and Cabinet (DPC) and the NSW Treasury. It was established to work with its partners and facilitate growth in the SII market. As of 2018, the OSII has supported six impact investments valued at over AUD200 million to provide better services for 16,000 people and families in NSW (OSII, 2018). Other states have also been involved in a variety of initiatives ranging from administering social enterprise grants schemes; developing SIIs for particular social programmes; creating social enterprise networks; and progressing various SII discussion papers, studies and strategies.

Australian Taskforce on Social Impact Investing

The Australian Taskforce comprises an independent Expert Panel with SII expertise and a support team within the Department of the Prime Minister and Cabinet. The Taskforce's interim report (2019) provided a set of recommendations and policy initiatives which outline the government's potential role in the SII market. The final report of the Australian Taskforce has not yet been publicly released.

Adapting from the GSG (2018) report on the role of government in catalysing the impact investment ecosystem, the Australian Taskforce on Social Impact Investing report (2019, p. 9) envisages a prominent role for government in stimulating the development of the SII market, particularly in the following areas:

> *Market facilitation.* Government has a public policy role to play in the creation of organisations and systems that support an efficient and effective SII market. Examples include the establishment of Big Society Capital in the UK and the creation of the OSII in NSW.
>
> *Market regulator.* Government is responsible for legislation and regulations that affect all markets, including the SII market. For example, governments oversee legislation on the corporate structure of social enterprises, fiduciary duties for investors and tax and fiscal incentives.
>
> *Market participant.* Government can participate in the market as a purchaser of social outcomes. Increasingly, governments are exploring outcome-based payments as an alternative to grant funding for organisations to deliver social services. Governments can also support social enterprise through procurement policy.[23]

The GSG report examined several countries, including Australia, in terms of how it is performing in its role as market facilitator, market participant and market regulator. This is summarised in Figure 5.1 which highlights the differences between existing policies and policies that are in progress. The y-axis of Figure 5.1 describes the market building contribution of government as a market facilitator, market participant/procurer and market regulator/legislator. The x-axis in Figure 5.1 describes market participants in terms of (1) demand for impact capital, (2) intermediaries (which facilitate the exchange of impact capital between the supply and demand side and might include funds, impact investment wholesalers and social stock exchanges), (3) suppliers of impact capital and (4) ecosystem enabler (actors who facilitate the impact ecosystem, without necessarily providing capital. These range from financial advisors to research centres or NABs) (see GSG, 2018, p. 3).

Figure 5.1 identifies existing government policies in place for 'access to capital' (as a market participant on the supply side), 'capacity building' (as a market facilitator on the demand side), 'outcomes commissioning' (as a market participant on the demand side), 'educational programs' (as a market facilitator on the ecosystem enabler side) and 'private sector NAB membership' (as a market facilitator on the ecosystem enabler side). However, there are no existing policies (or rather policies are in progress) in place for 'impact reporting standards' (as a market regulator where impact reporting standards are relevant to all market participants), 'impact in fiduciary duty' (as a market regulator on the supply side), 'impact in procurement' (as a market facilitator on the demand side), 'wholesaler' (as a market facilitator for

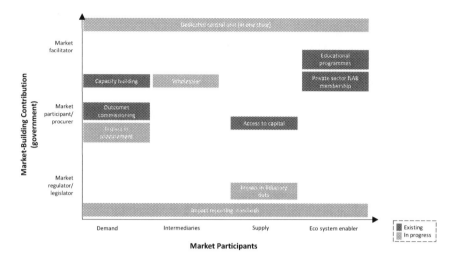

FIGURE 5.1 Social impact investment policies in Australia

Source: GSG report (2018, p. 22)

intermediaries) and 'dedicated central unit (in one state)' (as a market facilitator relevant to all market participants).

In terms of 'access to capital' in Figure 5.1, the GSG (2018, pp. 23–24) report noted that the federal government has been catalysing impact investment in areas such as affordable housing, through the National Housing Finance and Investment Corporation (NHFIC). The National Housing Infrastructure Facility (NHIF) provides financial assistance to registered community housing providers, state or territory governments or government-owned development corporations or utility providers, local government authorities and other parties to invest in critical infrastructure to accelerate the supply of housing, particularly affordable housing.[24] Another example is the Clean Energy Finance Corporation (CEFC). The CEFC is a statutory authority established under the Clean Energy Finance Corporation Act (2012) (the 'CEFC Act') which has a mission of reducing Australia's carbon missions. The CEFC is responsible for investing AUD10 billion in clean energy projects (such as renewable energy, energy efficiency and low emissions opportunities) over ten years on behalf of the Australian government. Other initiatives include the Indigenous Business Australia (IBA), a Commonwealth Government agency which encourage impact investment in ventures that support Indigenous economic development.[25]

Capacity building is another area in Figure 5.1 where the federal government has existing policies which support SII. At the national level, the Australian government's 2017–2018 budget provided AUD30 million over ten years to support social impact investment in Australia (and a further AUD6.7 million in the 2018–2019 budget). Of the 2017–2018 budget, AUD7.48 million was allocated to support the Sector Readiness Fund (SRF). This fund provides capability-building grants to non-government impact-driven businesses bringing new social investments to the market.[26] The Pacific Readiness for Investment in Social Enterprise (Pacific RISE) is a pilot innovation of the Australian government. According to its website:

> Pacific RISE, a program funded by the Australian Government's Department of Foreign Affairs and Trade (DFAT), was designed to pilot and facilitate a social impact market in the Pacific with the aim of delivering greater economic empowerment in the Pacific, particularly for women.[27]

In terms of outcome commissioning (or outcomes contracting), governments in NSW, Victoria, Queensland and South Australia have all commissioned SIBs, particularly in NSW which the OSII has committed to a number of SIBs (discussed in Chapter 4). A further example is the Social and Affordable Housing Fund (SAHF), established by the NSW government, which takes an innovative approach to the delivery of social and affordable housing in NSW, including the use of outcome-based contracts.[28]

While Figure 5.1 indicates there are no current government policies relating to 'fiduciary duties' of trustees, they are currently under consideration in Australia. For instance, the Financial System Inquiry (FSI) (2014), established by the Federal Treasurer, the Hon. Joe Hockey, made certain recommendation relating to the SII market in Australia. According to the Terms of Reference, the objective of the FSI (2014, p. vii):

> The Inquiry is charged with examining how the financial system could be positioned to best meet Australia's evolving needs and support Australia's economic growth. Recommendations will be made that foster an efficient, competitive and flexible financial system, consistent with financial stability, prudence, public confidence and capacity to meet the needs of users.

Recommendation 32 of the FSI (2014, p. 261) specifically addressed social impact investing:

> Explore ways to facilitate development of the impact investment market and encourage innovation in funding social service delivery.
>
> Provide guidance to superannuation trustees on the appropriateness of impact investment.
>
> Support law reform to classify a private ancillary fund as a 'sophisticated' or 'professional' investor, where the founder of the fund meets those definitions.

While no legislative changes have been made yet, the Australian Prudential and Regulatory Authority's (APRA) Prudential Practice Guide SPG 530 'Investment Governance' does leave the door open for the superannuation industry to potentially invest in SIIs. However, as discussed in Chapter 8, the cautionary tone of SPG 530 could dissuade fund managers from engaging in social impact investing. APRA and the government could remove this uncertainty altogether by explicitly encouraging SII as a desirable investment strategy for the superannuation industry.

In terms of a 'dedicated central unit', the GSG (2018, p. 5) report defines this as 'a centre of expertise within the government, that withstands changing administrations, to develop and oversee impact investing policies'. While the State of NSW has a dedicated OSII, the federal government does not currently have a department or agency with overall responsibility for social impact investing in this country.

In terms of future initiatives, the GSG (2018) highlighted the importance of establishing a wholesaler financial institution such as Impact Capital Australia (akin to Big Society Capital in the UK) as proposed by the AAB and Impact Investing Australia (see Addis et al., 2015). If established, Impact Capital Australia could play a vital role in facilitating the broader SII market in Australia in similar vein to how Big Society Capital has been highly effective in promoting the UK social investment market. However, the Australian government has still not committed to this proposal.

Other recommendations include: (1) expanding government procurement practices from impact businesses; legalising B (Benefit) Corporations in Australia (as legal status for impact-driven organisations will help with targeted government policy around impact business development; (2) build on the existing recommendations to encourage the incorporation of environmental, social and governance (ESG) factors into decision-making, likely through legislation, to help enable investment into impact assets; (3) create more fiscal incentives for impact investment; (4) work towards the establishment of a standardised impact reporting framework; and (5) encourage the incorporation of non-financial factors to reporting standards (see GSG, 2018, p. 24).

Challenges to the SII market

While there is wide international acceptance of the importance of the SII market from many foundations, regulators and investment funds, there are significant headwinds to the development of SII markets. As previously stated, there is a significant mismatch between investor enthusiasm and appetite for impact investing and the actual amount of capital invested to date. Unlike public companies, social enterprises will find it harder to access capital because of the absence of expert intermediaries and secondary markets, perception of high risk and lack of effective regulation and regulatory oversight governing the SII market. While there has been a level of government commitment to various SII initiatives, government needs to play a much larger role as a market facilitator, a market regulator and a market participant to grow the SII market. As seen in Figure 5.1, there are several areas where the government could be playing a more active role in developing the SII market.

From our literature review, there are many challenges facing the growth of the SII market. Many of these challenges reflect the nascent and early stages of the SII market, and include:

Limited Investment Opportunities. In theory, SIIs can embrace any asset class, geographical location, investment style or risk–return scenario. However, in reality, there are currently very limited impact investment opportunities available. In Australia, there are limited opportunities to make SIIs through secondary markets (such as social stock exchanges or impact investment wholesalers) or through over the counter transactions. There is also a lack of expert intermediaries who can facilitate and structure social impact transactions or impact funds who can invest in social enterprises on behalf of impact investors. Large investors, in particular, require investment diversification opportunities at scale to increase returns and reduce risk.

Small and Illiquid Investments. Consistent with the nascent nature of the SII market, investments opportunities tend to be small in scale and illiquid (i.e. privately rather than publicly traded) in nature. There is also a lack of clear exit strategies for many of these investments as the SII cannot readily be sold on any actively traded market.[29]

Cost and Complexity. Social impact investments, such as SIBs, can be costly and time-consuming to set up. They also involve negotiations with several market participants (such as investors, service providers and government) who need to agree on the social outcomes to be delivered. These outcomes also need to be rigorously measured and independently evaluated. This adds to the cost and complexity of these transactions.

Need for Robust Measurement. According to the Australian Taskforce on Social Impact Investing, only around two thirds of Australian social enterprises measure their social impact. As discussed in Chapter 7, some level of consensus among market participants is needed for measuring and evaluating social impact which is critical to the overall success of SII investments. Robust measurement and reporting are also important to prevent 'impact washing', where claimed social impact can be exaggerated or at least not proven. The problems underlying measurement are highlighted by the Australian Taskforce on Social Impact Investing report (2019, p. 23) which states: 'Australian social entrepreneurs have indicated that their ability to measure their impact is constrained by limited resources and the need to meet requirements of a variety of stakeholders'.

Also as stated by Trelstad (2016a, para. 2):

> Currently, impact can mean anything from venture investments in new health technologies to microfinance loans in Peru; from affordable housing in the US to renewable energy in India; from social impact bonds to private equity funds that create jobs. That's just the beginning of the confusion – even if you accepted that such diverse investments should all be grouped into one category, how do you even measure and compare impact anyway?

Lack of Good Quality Data. According to the Australian Taskforce, any measurement framework needs to be supported by the best quality data on social impact, in the absence of which impact reporting is not feasible. While the quality and availability of impact data has improved in recent years, many challenges remain. Large government datasets, in particular, can be complex to integrate, of variable quality, and difficult to access. A lack of quality data to measure and quantify many social outcomes can undermine investor confidence in the SII market. Determining the cost of social programs is also an essential factor in the pricing of social service delivery, the quantification and monetisation of rates of returns for investors and the assessment of risk (discussed in Chapter 4).

Insufficient Evidence on Realised Benefits and Value for Money. According to the Ernst and Young (EY) report (2016), there is limited evidence of realised financial benefits for government, both nationally and internationally, primarily due to the developing nature of the sector and the early stage of many existing SIIs. While SIIs provide examples of positive performance and savings to government, the overall evidence is limited as many instruments are not mature, while impact reporting is not consistent and may be selectively biased. While the EY report found some positive indicators of benefit to the Australian government in this nascent but rapidly growing sector, the evidence base is still maturing and will require continued monitoring and incorporation of lessons learned to date.

In addition to some of the concerns above, the OSII identifies other barriers to the growth of the SII market in NSW, including limited proven models to build investor confidence, diverse views on how to measure outcomes, the need for government to see genuine risk-sharing in transactions and sufficient capability and capacity across government and social sector organisations.

Key points from Chapter 5

Australian federal and state governments have taken a number of important steps to promote the Australian SII market.

In 2017, the Commonwealth Treasury established a number of SII principles for guiding federal government activity and initiatives in the emerging SII market including (1) government as market enabler and developer, (2) value for money, (3) robust outcome-based measurement and evaluation, (4) fair sharing of risk and return, (5) outcomes that align with the Australian government's policy priorities and (6) co-design.

A number of federal government entities are now involved in SII activity, including Department of Social Services, IBA, Department of Foreign Affairs and Trade, Department of Industry, Innovation and Science, CEFC and the NHFIC.

As part of the 2019–2020 budget, the federal government established a Taskforce on Social Impact Investing to examine the government's role in the SII market.

Many of the Taskforce's recommendations and strategies are similar to other international initiatives, particularly the G8 Taskforce on Social Impact Investment (launched under the UK's presidency of the G8) and the GSG (2018) report.

The purpose of the Australian Taskforce is to identify a way forward for federal government investments in SII, including how SII can provide solutions to some of society's most intractable social problems.

The Taskforce envisages that government has an important role to play in the broader development of the SII market including as a market facilitator, a market regulator and a market participant.

There have also been a number of developments at the state and territory levels of government, for example, NSW has a dedicated OSII.

There are many challenges facing the growth of the SII market including limited investment opportunities, small and illiquid markets, cost and complexity of SII transactions (such as SIBs), need for robust measurement frameworks, lack of good quality data on social issues and insufficient evidence on realised benefits and value for money.

Notes

1 The G8 is the Group of Eight industrialised nations including Canada, France, Germany, Italy, Japan, Russia, the UK and the US. However, the G8 reverted back to the G7 when Russia permanently departed the G8 in 2014.

2 David Cameron Prime Minister, UK World Economic Forum, Davos, 2013. Cited from Kamal Ahmed (2013).

3 See background at www.impactstrategist.com/case-studies/australian-advisory-board-on-impact-investing (viewed 19 June 2021).

4 For the SII market to be successful and reach it goals, the G8 Taskforce report (2014) also challenged the role of traditional investment analysis based on risk and return. For instance, the report recommended a rethinking and refocusing of the traditional risk–return framework to include the third dimension of impact, creating the *risk–return–impact* framework. While analytical frameworks based on the risk–return–impact dynamic are in the very early stages, at least one study by Saltuk (2012) proposed a portfolio management tool to analyse impact investments across these three dimensions including a graphical interface to 'set targets, map investments and aggregate the profile of the portfolio as a whole' (p. 1). Emerson (2003) also challenged the traditional view of investment returns as a trade-off between financial and social interest but rather advocates for a blended value proposition which integrates social and financial returns. He stated (p. 38):

> What is required is a unifying framework that expands the definition of investment and return beyond the historic one of finance and toward a new definition capable of holding a broader understanding of value than that most frequently reflected in traditionally endorsed financial operating ratios. In truth, the core nature of investment and return is not a trade off between social and financial interest but rather the pursuit of an embedded value proposition composed of both.

5 A number of other more specific recommendations of the G8 Taskforce (2014) report (pp. 17, 26, 33, 38) included providing capability-building grants for social sector organisations (Recommendation 1, p. 17); creating legal forms or regulations that protect the social mission of impact-driven businesses (Recommendation 2, p. 17);

relaxing regulations that prevent social sector organisations from generating revenues (Recommendation 3, p. 17); improve access of impact entrepreneurs to capital, including seed, early-stage and growth capital (Recommendation 4, p. 17); broadening use of outcome-based government commissioning (Recommendation 5, p. 17); introducing regulatory and tax incentives for impact investment (Recommendation 1, p. 27); defining fiduciary duty of foundation and pension fund trustees to allow investment in impact assets (Recommendation 2, p. 27); supporting specialist intermediaries that manage impact capital and develop impact investment products and services (Recommendation 3, p. 27); making impact products accessible to retail pension and savings investors (Recommendation 4, p. 27); establishing a social impact investment wholesaler, potentially financed through unclaimed assets, to serve as market champion and help it create specialist investment intermediaries (Recommendation 5, p. 27); allowing Foundations and philanthropists to allocate a percentage of their endowments or wealth to achieving impact (Recommendation 6, p. 27); supporting a single impact accounting system that incorporates existing initiatives by GRI, SASB, GIIN, the EU and GIIRS (Recommendation 1, p. 33); publishing data on the costs to government of social issues (Recommendation 2, p. 33); supporting standardised measurement of social impact to appear alongside financial performance metrics (Recommendation 3, p. 33); Foundations to use grant capital to help impact-driven organisations build up the capacity to measure impact (Recommendation 4, p. 33); government adoption of impact measurement in reporting and contracting requirements (Recommendation 5, p. 33); supporting coordination and collaboration between DFIs and their private sector agencies to advance impact investment (Recommendation 1, p. 38); exploring impact funds to support small- and medium-sized firms and those serving bottom of the pyramid customers (Recommendation 2, p. 38); allowing development finance institutions to increase impact investment efforts (Recommendation 3, p. 38); exploring the creation of an Impact Finance Facility to provide early-stage risk capital (Recommendation 4, p. 38; encouraging governments to explore how SIBs and DIBs might contribute to efficiency of social service delivery (Recommendation 5, p. 38); exploring the creation of a DIB Social Outcomes Fund to pay for successful DIBs (Recommendation 6, p. 38).

6 The G8 Taskforce report (2014, p. 42) suggested this can be achieved by creating a social investment wholesaler to act as a market champion, potentially financed by unclaimed assets in bank accounts, insurance companies and pension funds; considering early-stage support to specialist impact investment funds, intermediaries and advisory firms; supporting efforts to establish a 'kitemark' or labelling system that identifies social finance products for particular segments of the market; supporting efforts to enable access to a social stock exchange; and promoting the use and development of innovative impact finance products.

7 Such as providing matching finance to pump-prime the impact investment market or provide first loss facilities and other guarantees and so on (see G8 Taskforce report, p. 44).

8 Other initiatives recommended by the G8 Taskforce included reducing the restrictions on retail investors engaging in impact investing, e.g. through crowdfunding and other measures, defining fiduciary duty of foundation and pension fund trustees to allow investment in impact assets and investigating how impact investments can be integrated into existing regulatory frameworks covering banks, insurance companies and investment funds (see G8 Taskforce report, p. 42).

9 https://gsgii.org/leaders-declaration-for-a-just-and-sustainable-future (viewed 19 June 2021).

10 Note that the Canadian Taskforce report developed on the 2010 recommendations of the Canadian Task Force on Social Finance which focused on mobilising new sources of capital, creating an enabling tax and regulatory environment and building a pipeline of investment-ready social enterprises. Similar to the findings of the G8 Taskforce, the Canadian Taskforce findings suggest that the SII market will only succeed if all market participants come together, often with the help of intermediaries, to design new products, policies and impact measurement methods and to galvanise both supply and demand side development.

11 According to its website, Social Ventures Australia is a

> social purpose organisation that works with partners to improve the lives of people in need. We focus on keys to overcoming disadvantage in Australia, including great education, sustainable jobs, stable housing and appropriate health, disability and community services. Our range of services are designed to scale social impact, helping business, government and philanthropists to be more effective funders and social purpose organisation to be more effective at delivering services.

See https://mk0socialventuraff85.kinstacdn.com/assets/SVA-Fundamentals-for-Impact-2-pager-web.pdf) (viewed 19 June 2021).

12 For instance, Impact Investing Australia (2015) published a Blueprint to Market: Impact Capital Australia, written by Rosemary Addis, Sally McCutchan and Peter Munro. According to the proposal, the creation of Impact Capital Australia (ICA)

> would have two roles: investor and market champion. The focus of ICA's investment activity would predominantly be wholesale, as a supporter of existing and new intermediaries. It would also originate socially impactful, innovative and scalable solutions and ways of funding and financing them. It would be a proactive market builder to accelerate growth and impact by identifying opportunities and removing barriers.

13 See https://treasury.gov.au/programs-initiatives-consumers-community/social-impact-investing/australian-government-principles-for-social-impact-investing (viewed 19 June 2021).

14 See https://treasury.gov.au/programs-initiatives-consumers-community/social-impact-investing/australian-government-principles-for-social-impact-investing (viewed 19 June 2021).

15 See https://treasury.gov.au/programs-initiatives-consumers-community/social-impact-investing/australian-government-principles-for-social-impact-investing (viewed 19 June 2021).

16 See https://treasury.gov.au/programs-initiatives-consumers-community/social-impact-investing/australian-government-principles-for-social-impact-investing (viewed 19 June 2021).

17 See https://treasury.gov.au/programs-initiatives-consumers-community/social-impact-investing/australian-government-principles-for-social-impact-investing (viewed 19 June 2021).

18 See https://treasury.gov.au/programs-initiatives-consumers-community/social-impact-investing/australian-government-principles-for-social-impact-investing (viewed 19 June 2021).

19 See https://treasury.gov.au/programs-initiatives-consumers-community/social-impact-investing/australian-government-principles-for-social-impact-investing (viewed 19 June 2021).

20 The strategy outlines three key focus areas of targeted support to address the challenges social enterprises face: (1) building capability and capacity in the sector including access to financial support, (2) making connections across the sector to increase collaboration and promotional opportunities and (3) improving market access by linking social enterprises to procurement opportunities. See https://desbt.qld.gov.au/small-business/strategic-documents/social-enterprise-strategy (viewed 19 June 2021).

21 The Queensland 2020–2021 State Budget provided AUD8 million over two years for the Social Enterprise Jobs Fund 'to support social enterprises to scale-up activities and create training and employment opportunities'. See https://desbt.qld.gov.au/small-business/strategic-documents/social-enterprise-strategy (viewed 19 June 2021).

22 According to its website, this Network 'was established in early 2018 to build a connected community of social enterprises, to facilitate access to learning and development opportunities, and to give practitioners an independent and collective voice' (see https://senvic.org.au/about-senvic) (viewed 19 June 2021).

23 The Australian Taskforce on Social Impact Investing adapted this model from the Global Steering Group for Impact Investment (2018).

24 More information can be found at the NHFIC website: www.nhfic.gov.au/media/1576/nhif-fact-sheet.pdf (viewed 19 June 2021).

25 More information can be found at the IBA website: https://iba.gov.au (viewed 19 June 2021).

26 More information can be found at the SRF website: www.communitygrants.gov.au/grants/sector-readiness-fund-%E2%80%93-fund-administrator-activity (viewed 19 June 2021).

27 See Pacific Rise website: www.pacificrise.org/about (viewed 19 June 2021).

28 See SAHF website: www.facs.nsw.gov.au/about/reforms/future-directions/initiatives/SAHF (viewed 19 June 2021).

29 The OECD (2019, p. 104) report also noted differences in time horizons between investor expectations and social impact investments:

> However, across regions, studies indicate that small and medium-sized enterprises (SMEs) and entrepreneurs face a 'missing middle' for those seeking to scale-up and expand their operations. In addition, the time frame for many enterprises to reach sustainability and scale are often longer than the investors first expected and this needs to be taken into account in thinking about follow-on financing rounds.

6

TOWARDS A VIABLE SII MARKET IN AUSTRALIA

Introduction

In this chapter, we discuss critical factors necessary to promote an active and viable Australian social impact investing (SII) market. We argue that in order for Australia to develop a transparent, liquid and efficient SII market, the market needs many more expert intermediaries capable of facilitating, coordinating and managing social impact investments (such as Social Ventures Australia [SVA] and Social Finance in the UK) and a social stock exchange (SSE) to facilitate SII deals and transactions between social enterprises and investors. We discuss some notable examples of social stock exchange platforms around the world which have been established to provide an active marketplace for both primary and secondary transactions including the provision of information for investors on potential investment opportunities. Further, if secondary markets for social impact investments are to be efficient and effective and build investor confidence, there also needs to be high-quality regulation and oversight, including effective corporate governance, transparency and risk evaluation metrics comparable to listed public companies. In a social impact bond (SIB) arrangement, for example, government payments are only made when the social service provider achieves the agreed social outcomes. One of the key risks for an investor is that the service provider, whether it be a private company, a non-government organisation (NGO) or a not-for-profit (NFP) entity, fails to deliver on the agreed social outcomes. To protect investors and promote market efficiency, we suggest that rigorous risk evaluation tools are needed so that market participants can evaluate the financial viability, performance and service delivery capability of social service providers and social enterprises more generally. We review aspects of the corporate distress prediction literature and conclude that while most distress prediction models have been applied to publicly listed companies, they can be readily adapted to

DOI: 10.4324/9781003225591-6

private companies, NGOs and NFP entities engaged in social service delivery. We also suggest that service providers responsible for social service delivery require effective assurance and governance frameworks to ensure greater accountability, transparency and social delivery effectiveness. We propose to integrate the various risk factors discussed in this chapter into an overall scoring model or rating system that can be used to assess the viability and performance of service providers.

Factors influencing the growth of SII market in Australia

While Australia has one of the most mature SII markets in the region (and possibly the world), the market is only in its most formative stages. Ultimately, the Australian Taskforce on Social Impact Investing report (2019, p. 22)

> envisages a future in which Australia has a deep capital market for social impact investments facilitated by skilled specialist advisor 'intermediaries', with measurable social and financial returns across a broad range of investments – from those with a low to those with a market-rate of financial return.

With these ambitious targets in mind (and the realisation that this vision is likely some time away), the Australian Taskforce proposed recommendations to create more impact investing opportunities for investors. However, a great deal more government action is required to ensure the underlying structure and regulatory frameworks are established to support an efficient and effective SII market that can build investor confidence and promote the overall integrity of the market.

For the Australian SII market to grow and meet the Taskforce's vision for growth, an SII market needs expert intermediaries capable of facilitating, coordinating and structuring social impact investments. For example, SVA is an NFP organisation active in developing the SIB market and partners with social service providers and governments to structure SIB transactions.[1] Social Finance in the UK performs a similar role in the SII market and was one of the first innovators of the SIB (discussed in Chapter 5).

An SII market also needs well-functioning secondary markets comparable to mainstream capital markets with a similar level of high-quality regulation and oversight. This requires more comprehensive regulation covering issues such as corporate governance, periodic and continuous disclosure, generally agreed-upon concepts of impact measurement, comprehensive social outcome evaluation frameworks and rigorous risk assessment tools and assurance and governance frameworks for service providers.

Promoting a Social Stock Exchange in Australia

One way to attract social impact investors, increase liquidity and access and provide exit strategies for impact investments is to promote a secondary market such as an social stock exchange in Australia. Social stock exchanges are a relatively new concept (see Wendt, 2020). They allow publicly listed impact-driven businesses to be connected to investors who are seeking to generate positive impact alongside a financial return.

According to Chhichhia (2015, paras. 1–2):

> Markets and socialism have been strange bedfellows since the start of the industrial revolution, and until recently, most of us have considered them mutually exclusive states of affairs. That is about to change. A third dimension is slowly finding its place in traditional market dichotomy – a dimension that includes social business, impact investing, and now social stock exchanges (SSEs). Social businesses, in their many forms, have been around for a while, but the latest trend seems to be SSEs – trading platforms listing only social businesses. Using SSEs, investors can buy shares in a social business just as investors focused solely on profit would do in the traditional stock market. An investor would come to an SSE to find a social business with a mission according to his or her preference. This is great news for all players in the industry (including governments, multilateral financing institutions, community organizations, development agencies, and social entrepreneurs), and countries like Canada, the UK, Singapore, South Africa, Brazil, and Kenya have already opened their doors to their very own social stock exchanges.

Wendt (2020, pp. 91–94) provided a useful summary of the views drawn from practitioners about the potential benefits and practicalities of a social stock exchange. We paraphrase some of her points as follows: (1) SSEs can improve market access for social enterprises by bringing together impact-driven businesses with investors who are seeking financial returns combined with social impact; (2) SSEs can become hubs of information for investors. By aggregating data on impact-driven companies and organising analyst coverage, SSEs can reduce information asymmetries and transaction costs while facilitating more robust valuation of the listed companies; (3) SSEs can provide a company a 'seal of quality', providing investors with confidence that appropriate due diligence processes have been adopted and there is adequate governance and transparency around the company's affairs; (4) without the availability of a liquid investment market, impact investors may lean towards being excessively cautious, or avoid investment altogether, which will limit the amount of capital available to impact-driven companies. Social stock exchanges can also provide avenues for an exit strategy for early-stage investors which will ultimately make impact investments more attractive to investors; (5) SSEs can introduce market discipline and encourage competition between impact companies. In a similar way that stock exchanges provide an important regulatory function, SSEs can facilitate the more developed regulatory frameworks for impact investing; (6) by making impact investing more accessible and popular, SSEs can increase investment for sustainable development, both in developed and in developing countries; (7) SSEs can help the sector to transition into a more regulated capital market, regulated by an SSE board which can 'help avoid mission drift, focus attention on

UN SDGs, and help their implementation while eliminating market inefficiencies' (see Wendt, 2020, p. 94).

There are some notable international examples of social impact exchange platforms around the world which have been established to provide a marketplace for both primary and secondary transactions including the provision of information on potential investment opportunities to investors (see Chhichhia, 2015). We briefly describe them below.

The UK Social Stock Exchange

The UK Social Stock Exchange (SSX) was established in June 2013. The first few companies to become members listed on the SSX included Ashley House plc, V22 plc, Straight plc, Scope, Places for People, ITM Power plc, ValiRx plc, Good Energy Group plc, Primary Health Properties plc, Halosource plc and Accsys Technologies plc. At the time of listing, these companies were engaged in industries such as social and affordable housing, clean technology, waste, water, recycling, renewable energy, sustainable transport, health, education and culture.

The SSX is also supported by high-profile organisations including the London Stock Exchange Group, City of London Corporation, Big Society Capital and the Rockefeller Foundation. While the SSX is not a regulated stock exchange, and is not involved in actual share trading, it has a rigorous three-stage process for admission including (1) the requirement to be admitted to a regulated stock exchange such as the London Stock Exchange; (2) the production of an Impact Report detailing how well the business has performed against key social performance targets; and (3) an assessment of social impact by the SSX's admissions panel, formed of leading SII experts.

Independent experts conduct the review and publish an SSX Impact Report covering:

- The social or environmental mission of the social business
- Target beneficiaries
- How a company's products, services and operations deliver social impact
- How a company involves and consults with all of its stakeholders
- Evidence of social impact and how it is measured and reported

The SSX partners with London's ICAP Securities and Derivatives Exchange (ISDX) and serves as a directory of companies that have met the screening process. The SSX also acts as a research service for impact investors. An obvious advantage of being listed on the SSX is that it provides social enterprises visibility and access to a wide network of impact investors.

Canada's Social Venture Connexion (SVX)

The Social Venture Connexion (SVX) was established in September 2013 and is a single-access point platform for ventures, funds and investors seeking social and/or environmental impact alongside financial return. According to SVX (2020, paras. 1–2):

> An enterprise should intend to create a direct impact through a business model that aims to tackle a market shortfall, problem, or externality … We also work with conscious companies that may not have impact objectives as the driving force of the company, but they intend to improve existing conditions. They may aim to use responsible principles in their procurement, production, distribution channels, environmental footprint, worker rights, and community … Although Corporate Social Responsibility approaches are positive, we do not believe in driving impact where social benefit is ancillary or reliant on profits. Impact must be core to what our issuers do.

All products on the SVX platform are Canadian private market securities. The SVX uses crowdfunding and direct placement to support capital raising by impact ventures and funds. Investors and issuers can manage their investments and make transactions using the SVX platform and have 24-hour access to all documents in one place. The SVX allows entrepreneurs to list a company and its securities, customise the fundraising page and bring on investors.

Singapore's Impact Investment Exchange (IIX)

The Impact Investment Exchange (IIX) opened in June 2013 and is the only public social stock exchange. It functions similar to the UK SSX by providing information about social businesses and impact investing funds. It also includes NFPs in its list of issuers which can issue debt securities such as bonds. According to the IIX (2020, para. 1), it provides

> unique expertise across the value chain of sustainable investing, our products and platforms unlock large scale capital from investors, help grow inclusive businesses, measure impact created on the ground, advise and design solutions to achieve sustainability goals, and bridge knowledge gaps through education and research.

South Africa's Social Investment Exchange (SASIX)

The South African Social Investment Exchange (SASIX) opened in June 2006 in an attempt to provide finance to social businesses. It is online and offers ethical investors a platform to buy shares in social projects according to two classifications: sector and province. Organisations that are achieving a measurable social impact are selected to list on the exchange. Investors can make a contribution for as little as R50 per share. According to SASIX (2017 paras. 1–2):

> The South African Social Investment Exchange provides independent research, evaluation and monitoring to ensure that listed projects meet a

set of criteria, including the ability to deliver measurable returns whether these are social or financial or a combination of both. SASIX applies the same sort of due diligence consideration to projects as would be applied to purely financial investments, including assessing need and evaluating depth, breadth, permanence, strengths and risks. Our process is underpinned by detailed sector and best practice research. This clarifies how we identify and target the social investment areas and, within these, the activities we recommend. Our research has focused on priority development sectors, chosen specifically for their alignment to the Millennium Development Goals, as well as their national and regional significance in the lives of people and communities.

If secondary markets for SII are to be effective and attract investor confidence and participation, there must be high-quality regulation and oversight, including effective corporate governance and transparency. For instance, the Australian Stock Exchange (ASX) has listing rules which cover detailed disclosure requirements, continuous disclosure, significant transactions, corporate governance and the application of Australian accounting and auditing standards. There are also extensive regulations flowing from the Corporations Act 2001. Also needed are well-developed credit risk models for assessing the risk and solvency of service providers and social enterprises. The remainder of this chapter considers these issues.

The need for more rigorous risk evaluation tools

For public companies, there are a wide range of risk models that regulators, auditors, creditors and investors can use to assess risk and financial performance. These tools are critical to the operation of a transparent and well-functioning capital market. Risk evaluation models are used in many important contexts including (1) by banks and lending institutions in decisions to extend a loan to company, and in the ongoing assessment of loan security; (2) by auditors in evaluating a company's ability to continue as a going concern, or whether it can continue to meet its obligations as they fall due into the foreseeable future; (3) by investors in understanding the risk and return dynamic of their investments; and (4) by fund managers and investment banks in the measurement of portfolio risk, and in the pricing of defaultable bonds, credit derivatives and other securities exposed to credit risk (Jones and Hensher, 2008).

The importance of risk evaluation tools for service providers (and social enterprises more broadly) can be illustrated in the case of SIIs. In an actively traded bond market, prices adjust quickly for changes in perceived risk factors (such as the financial distress of the bond issuer). For instance, if a corporate bond is perceived as riskier by investors, the bond will be sold-off. This reduces its price but raises the yield which compensates investors for the higher risk. However, SIIs operate in a largely illiquid market (i.e. they are not traded), and there is usually no market mechanism available to adjust price for changing risk factors.

In an SIB arrangement, for example, government payments are only made when the social service provider meets agreed social outcomes. One of the key risks for an investor is that the service provider, whether it be a private company, an NGO or an NFP entity, fails to deliver on the agreed social delivery targets or outcomes. There are also risks to government because even though the risk of service failure is effectively transferred to investors, the financial risk cannot be eliminated entirely. For instance, there can be lost progress payments if the SIB arrangement fails before the term of the bond. There is also potential reputational damage to the government for ultimately failing to provide an effective solution to the social issue at hand.

Predictive risk models are therefore needed to monitor the financial health of service providers. Most risk or distress models provide a probability of failure where a high probability score means that the company or service provider will either fail outright, experience distress or fail to meet its operating objectives (such as the delivery of social outcomes). Most distress prediction models identified in the literature have been applied to public companies, however many can be readily adapted to private companies, NGOs or NFP entities responsible for social service delivery.

Insolvency of charities, NGOs and NFPs

Charities, NGOs and NFPs can fail in the same way as a public company and can be wound up or have liquidators appointed. The Australian Charities and Not-for-Profits Commission (ACNC) (2020a, para. 1) employs a similar definition of insolvency as that used in the private sector and provides the following advice in the event of insolvency:

> A charity is insolvent when it is unable to pay all of its debts when they are due. A charity may be insolvent if it has overdue taxes, is behind on loan repayments, is operating at a loss, or is unable to pay for goods it has received.
> Generally speaking, charities that are insolvent must appoint a liquidator or administrator to manage the charity. In some cases, charities that are insolvent must be wound up. If an insolvent charity does not appoint an administrator or liquidator, a court may order it to be wound up (or liquidated).
>
> *ACNC, 2020a, para. 2*

In the financial distress literature, a variety of quantitative and qualitative frameworks have been utilised to predict financial distress or bankruptcy, although mainly for public companies. This section considers how useful and adaptable these models are to service providers engaged in social service delivery.

Financial distress prediction literature

Corporate distress prediction research has been prominent for the better part of four decades and still continues to attract much interest from academics, practitioners and regulators. Major economic collapses such as the 1997 Asian financial crisis, the 2001 'tech wreck', the global financial crisis (GFC) and, more recently, the global health crisis (GHC) arising from the COVID-19 pandemic have resulted in many more corporate failures across all sectors of the economy. In recent years, the much publicised collapse of large global corporations (such as Lehman brothers during the GFC and, more recently, companies such as Neiman Marcus, Hertz, JCPenny, Chesapeake during the GHC) has highlighted the significant economic, social and political costs associated with corporate failure. This has led to the development of a range of new distress prediction modelling approaches.

Distress prediction models typically take a set of input features or predictive variables and generate a probability or classification score based on those features. Variables that have a high association with distress (such as financial ratios) tend to provide better discriminating power between failing and healthy companies. Companies with weaker financial health tend to be associated with a higher probability of failure or distress.

Altman *Z* score model

The key objective in any distress prediction model is to identify the target distress variable. In corporate bankruptcy research, the target (or dependent variable) is usually a severe economic event, such as corporate bankruptcy or liquidation. For distress prediction research, the target variable is usually a solvency event, such as a creditor default or a forced capital restructure (such as getting better terms and conditions from a bank). As suggested above, many of these indicators can be applied to charities, NGOs and NFP entities. The ACNC also considers overdue taxes, being behind on loan repayments, operating at a loss, or being unable to pay for goods received, as indicators of potential insolvency.

The next step is to identify the independent or input variables in the model. These are the variables which the statistical model uses to predict the target variable (i.e. whether the firm goes bankrupt or, in the case of an NFP, whether it is likely to incur an operating loss or default on a creditor). The literature has found that a large number of predictor variables can have predictive power, such as financial ratios including profitability ratios, liquidity and solvency ratios and capital structure ratios such as debt equity. However, market variables and macro-economic factors have also been shown to have a strong influence in predicting failure.

One of the oldest and most famous distress prediction models is the Altman *Z* score model (Altman, 1968). In the Altman (1968) model above, five ratios were found to be particularly predictive of corporate bankruptcy: (1) working capital/ total assets (a measure of liquidity), (2) retained earnings/total assets (a measure of accumulated profitability and a proxy for the age of the company), (3) earnings before interest and tax/total assets (a measure of earnings generation capacity), (4) market value of equity/total liabilities (a measure of technical solvency or the extent that the market value of equity covers existing debt obligations) and (5) sales/ total assets (a measure of efficiency or the ability of the asset base to generate sales revenue). One can calculate the Altman *Z* score from five simple ratio measures:

$$Z \text{ score} = 1.2^\star(x_1) + 1.4^\star(x_2) + 3.3^\star(x_3) + 0.6^\star(x_4) + 1.0^\star(x_5)$$

where:

x_1 = working capital/total assets

x_2 = retained earnings/total assets

x_3 = earnings before interest and tax/total assets

x_4 = market value of equity/total liabilities

x_5 = sales/total assets (not in percentage terms)

According to Altman (1968), a Z score below 1.8 suggests the company is in finan-cial trouble, while companies with scores above 3 indicate a company is healthy. Because private companies do not have traded equity, the market value of equity is often replaced with the book value of equity to calculate the bankruptcy score.

One of the most important decisions in developing a distress model is the type of statistical learning model used to predict distress. Over the last 50 years, a large number of predictive models have been developed, ranging from relatively simplistic discrete choice models to advanced machined learning techniques. The Altman Z score model described above is an example of an early approach based on multiple discriminant analysis. More modern approaches include logit and probit modelling, advanced discrete choice (such as mixed logit, nested logit [NL] and latent class models), survival analysis and duration models, non-parametric techniques (particularly neural networks and recursive partitioning models), struc-tural models and reduced form (intensity) modelling. There have also been a number of important recent developments in artificial intelligence and machine learning (Jones, 2017).

Simple probability models

Logit and probit models are known as 'probability' models. They assume that for any firm, given a set of risk attributes, there is a definable probability that the firm will actually default on a loan or, in the case of service providers, fail in its ser-vice delivery function. This interpretation places all firms in a single population. The observed outcome (i.e. default/no default) arises from the characteristics and random behaviour of the firms. Ex ante, all that can be produced by the model is a probability (Jones and Hensher, 2008). According to Jones and Hensher (2008), the underlying logic of a distress prediction model is to ascertain how much a company resembles firms that have bankrupted or experienced financial distress in the past. These models provide a probability of failure given specified input variables.

Advanced probability models

The mixed logit approach is an example of a model that can accommodate firm-specific heterogeneity across firms through random parameters (Jones and Hensher, 2004). The essence of the approach is to decompose the stochastic error component into two additive (i.e. uncorrelated) parts. One part is correlated over alternative outcomes and is heteroscedastic, and another part is identically distributed error (IID) over alternative outcomes and firms (Jones and Hensher, 2008).

The major advantage of the mixed logit model is that it allows for the complete relaxation of highly restrictive statistical assumptions such as the independently and IIDs by allowing all unobserved variances and covariances to be different, up to identification. The model is highly flexible in representing sources of firm-specific observed and unobserved heterogeneity through the incorporation of random parameters (whereas multinomial logit [MNL] model and NL models only allow for *fixed* parameter estimates).

Jones and Hensher (2007) also present two other advanced form models, the NL model and the latent class multinomial (LCM) logit model. Both models are an improvement on the standard logit model but have quite different econometric properties from the mixed logit model. In essence, the NL model relaxes the severity of the MNL condition between subsets of alternatives but preserves the IID condition across alternatives within each nested subset. The popularity of the NL model arises from its close relationship to the MNL model. The authors argue that NL is essentially a set of hierarchical MNL models, linked by a set of conditional relationships. To take an example from Standard and Poor's credit ratings, we might have six alternatives, three of them Level A rating outcomes (AAA, AA, A, called the a-set) and three Level B rating outcomes (BBB, BB, B, called the b-set). The NL model is structured such that it predicts the probability of a particular Level A rating outcome conditional on a Level A rating. It also predicts the probability of a particular Level B rating outcome conditional on a Level B rating. Then the model predicts the probability of an A or a B outcome (called the c-set). That is, we have two lower level conditional outcomes and an upper level marginal outcome. Since each of the 'partitions' in the NL model is of the MNL form, they each display the IID condition between the alternatives within a partition. However, the variances are different between the partitions.

The main benefits of the NL model are its closed-form solution, which allows parameter estimates to be more easily estimated and interpreted, and a unique global set of asymptotically efficient parameter estimates. A relative weakness of the model is that it is analytical and conceptually closely related to MNL and therefore shares many of its limitations. NL only partially corrects for the highly restrictive IID condition and incorporates observed and unobserved heterogeneity to some extent only.[2]

Applying risk models to NFP service providers

While a large number of techniques have been developed to assess risk, there are comparatively few studies that can be applied to NFP entities. The main focus of predictive models is on public companies. Jones and Walker (2008) attempted to fill a gap in the distress literature by developing a quantitative modelling approach to explain and predict local government distress in Australia. As local government authorities typically do not fail *per se* (e.g. bankruptcy or loan default), a major objective for the authors was to develop a pragmatic and meaningful measure of local government distress that can be readily operationalised for statistical modelling purposes. Given the difficulties in finding an appropriate financial distress measure in local councils, Jones and Walker (2008) focus on constructing a proxy of distress linked to the basic operating objectives of local councils, which is to provide social services to the community. They operationalise this concept of distress in terms of an inability of local governments to provide social services at existing levels to the community.

In order to provide social services to the community, local governments are expected to invest in infrastructure and to maintain legacy infrastructure. Jones and Walker (2008) use the estimates developed by local governments of the cost of restoring infrastructure to a 'satisfactory condition' as a measure of degrees of 'distress'. As such, their study uses a quantitative measure of distress, as opposed to the more limited (and less relevant) binary classification that characterises private sector distress research.

The authors examine both qualitative and quantitative measures of service delivery and find that the qualitative measure provides a more explanatory and predictive indicator of distress. Using a latent class model, they find that in terms of higher impacts on council distress, the profile of latent Class 1 (which they call 'smaller lower revenue councils') is smaller councils servicing smaller areas that are relatively less affected by population levels but are highly impacted by road maintenance costs and lower revenue generation capacity (particularly rates revenue generation). In terms of higher impacts on council distress, the profile of latent Class 2 (which they call 'larger higher revenue councils') is larger councils servicing larger areas with higher population levels and lower full-time staff. These councils are less impacted by their rate revenue base but are highly impacted by lower overall revenue generation capacity. Compared to Class 1 councils, Class 2 councils are relatively less impacted by road programme costs and the carrying value of infrastructure assets. Jones and Walker (2008) also find that the classification accuracy of their LCM model is also higher than a standard multiple regression model.

Machine learning models

In more recent literature, machine learning models have proven very successful in distress prediction (Jones, 2017). The antecedents of modern boosting models come from the classification and regression trees (CART™) technique. However, despite the early popularity of CART™ (particularly in health diagnostics), the technique became associated with a number of limitations, most notably these models do not generalise (predict) well. More sophisticated boosting methodologies, such as random forests, adaptive boosting (AdaBoost) and gradient boosting, began to develop. Random forests are essentially a refined form of bagging. The technique improves on bagging by 'de-correlating' the trees, which maximises the reduction in variance (see Jones, 2017).[3]

Jones and Wang (2019) have developed a unique machine learning model to predict private company failure which can be readily applied to service providers in the NGO or NFP sectors. One of the more contentious issues in the literature has been the definition of private company failure. A wide range of failure definitions have been used across studies, including loss to borrowers and guarantee recipients, wound up by a court; liquidation or cessation of trading; sustained non-compliance with banking obligations; bankruptcy or liquidation; loan default; financial distress; bankruptcy or default; cash shortages; and a combination of bankruptcy, receivership, liquidation, inactive, special treatment firms (Jones and Wang, 2019).

Applying distress models to public sector, private companies and NFP entities engaged in service delivery is not without challenges (Jones and Walker, 2008). In the case of service providers in the private sector, it is a relatively straightforward process to develop distress prediction models based on large private company samples. Jones and Wang (2019) showed that quite good predictive models can be developed out-of-sample, even in quite complex multi-class settings involving varying types of distress. While it remains challenging to develop models for entities that do not have profit-making objectives, several approaches could prove fruitful.

One approach is to build prediction models for private companies (which do not have market characteristics) and apply the probabilities to social service delivery organisations. The model probabilities can be calibrated by size and industry groups to better profile NFP entities for the purpose of formulating more accurate predictions. It is possible to rank the distress probabilities from a private company model to generate a relative risk profile for organisations in the NFP sector.

Another approach suggested by Jones and Walker (2008) is to identify appropriate service delivery proxies for distress. The proxy could relate to the ability of an NFP to deliver social services effectively – for instance, not meeting key performance indicators in relation to service quantity or quality. For modelling purposes, these NFPs can be treated as distressed firms. While identifying a sufficiently large enough sample of poor performing NFPs might be challenging, this approach would provide the most direct way of monitoring the ongoing health of service providers.[4]

Assessing service providers: assurance and governance frameworks

In the sections above, we discussed various quantitative and empirical approaches for monitoring the financial health of the service provider using formal prediction models. However, there are also a number of qualitative factors that must be considered in assessing the efficacy and viability of an NGO or an NFP entity. Service providers also need effective assurance and governance frameworks to create and sustain investor confidence in the SII market. The fact that the NFP sector has been in the media spotlight recently for culpable activity and lax standards underscores the importance of robust assurance and governance frameworks.

NFP entities are not necessarily subject to the same robust oversight and monitoring rules as listed public companies which are subject to a plethora of different rules including ASX listing rules and the legislative requirements of Australian Securities and Investments Commission (ASIC). However, there have been recent attempts to improve regulation in the NFP sector. As stated by the Australian Institute of Company Directors in their 'Not-for-Profit Governance Principles' (2019, p. 3):

> Since that time, the sector has experienced significant regulatory reform and disruption. In recent years, great attention has been paid to the governance of not-for-profits and its role in maintaining the community's trust and in preventing misconduct, particularly against vulnerable people. It is fair to say that good governance has never been more important for the not-for-profit sector.

The ACNC Act 2012 governs the eligibility of an NFP entity to be registered as a charity for federal purposes and establishes the minimum governance standards and reporting requirements for registered charities and NFPs. In addition to the principles of the Australian Institute of Company Directors (discussed further below), the ACNC (2020b, paras. 6–10) Governance Standards set out five basic standards for the NFP sector as follows:

Standard 1: Purposes and not-for-profit nature. Charities must be not-for-profit and work towards their charitable purpose. They must be able to demonstrate this and provide information about their purposes to the public.

Standard 2: Accountability to members. Charities that have members must take reasonable steps to be accountable to their members and provide them with adequate opportunity to raise concerns about how the charity is governed.

Standard 3: Compliance with Australian laws. Charities must not commit a serious offence (such as fraud) under any Australian law or breach a law that may result in a penalty of 60 penalty units (equivalent to $12,600 as at December 2018) or more.

Standard 4: Suitability of Responsible Persons. Charities must take reasonable steps to: (a) Be satisfied that its Responsible Persons (such as board or committee members or trustees) are not disqualified from managing a corporation under the Corporations Act 2001 (Cth) or disqualified from being a Responsible Person of a registered charity by the ACNC Commissioner; and (b) Remove any Responsible Person who does not meet these requirements.

Standard 5: Duties of Responsible Persons. Charities must take reasonable steps to make sure that Responsible Persons are subject to, understand and carry out the duties set out in this Standard Under Governance Standard 5 a charity must take reasonable steps to make sure its responsible persons meet certain duties. These include to act with reasonable care and diligence, act honestly in the best interests of the charity and for its purposes, not misuse the position of responsible person, not to misuse information obtained in performing duties; disclose any actual or perceived conflict of interest; ensure that the charity's financial affairs are managed responsibly and not allow a charity to operate while insolvent.

The Australian Institute of Company Directors has also set out ten governance principles for the Directors of NFP entities as follows:[5]

Principle 1: purpose and strategy

- The organisation has a clear purpose and a strategy which aligns its activities with its purpose
- The organisation's purpose is clear, recorded in its governing documents and understood by the board
- The board approves a strategy to carry out the organisation's purpose
- Decisions by the board further the organisation's purpose and strategy
- The board regularly devotes time to consider strategy
- The board periodically reviews the purpose and strategy

Principle 2: roles and responsibilities

- There is clarity about the roles, responsibilities and relationships of the board
- Directors' roles are clear and understood by the board
- Directors understand and meet their duties under the law
- Directors meet any eligibility requirements relevant to their position
- Delegations of the board's authority are recorded and periodically reviewed
- The role of the board is clearly delineated from the role of management

Principle 3: board composition

- The board's structure and composition enable it to fulfil its role effectively
- Directors are appointed based on merit, through a transparent process, and in alignment with the purpose and strategy
- Tenure of directors is limited to encourage renewal and staggered to retain corporate knowledge
- The board reflects a mix of personal attributes which enable it to fulfil its role effectively
- The board assesses and records its members' skills and experience, and this is disclosed to stakeholders
- The board undertakes succession planning to address current and future skills needs in alignment with the purpose and the strategy

Principle 4: board effectiveness

- The board is run effectively, and its performance is periodically evaluated
- Board meetings are chaired effectively and provide opportunity for all directors to contribute
- Directors seek and are provided with the information they need to fulfil their responsibilities
- Directors are appropriately inducted and undertake ongoing education to fulfil their responsibilities
- The board's performance, as well as the performance of its chair and other directors, is periodically evaluated
- The relationship between the board and management is effective

Principle 5: risk management

- Board decision-making is informed by an understanding of risk and how it is managed
- The board oversees a risk management framework that aligns with the purpose and strategy
- Directors seek and are provided with information about risk and how it is managed
- The board periodically reviews the risk management framework

Principle 6: performance

- The organisation uses its resources appropriately and evaluates its performance
- The board oversees appropriate use of the organisation's resources
- The board approves an annual budget for the organisation
- The board receives and considers measures which evaluate performance against the strategy
- The board oversees the performance of the chief executive officer (CEO)
- The board monitors the solvency of the organisation

Principle 7: accountability and transparency

- The board demonstrates accountability by providing information to stakeholders about the organisation and its performance
- The organisation's governing documents and policies relevant to its governance are available to stakeholders
- The board oversees appropriate reporting to stakeholders about the organisation's performance and financial position
- Transactions between related parties, if any, are disclosed to stakeholders

- Directors' remuneration and other benefits, if any, are disclosed to stakeholders
- Members have the opportunity to ask questions about how the organisation is run and to hold the board to account for their decisions

Principle 8: stakeholder engagement

- There is meaningful engagement of stakeholders, and their interests are understood and considered by the board
- The board understands who the organisation's stakeholders are, their needs and their expectations
- The board oversees a framework for the meaningful engagement of stakeholders
- Stakeholders are considered in relevant board decision-making
- There is a process for gathering and responding to complaints and feedback from stakeholders
- The board oversees a framework for how the organisation works with and protects vulnerable people

Principle 9: conduct and compliance

- The expectations of behaviour for the people involved in the organisation are clear and understood
- The board articulates its expectations of conduct, and the consequences for misconduct, for the people involved with the organisation
- The board oversees compliance with relevant laws, regulations and internal policies
- Conflicts of interest are identified, disclosed and managed
- There is a process for investigating misconduct and relevant instances are brought to the attention of the board

Principle 10: culture

- The board models and works to instil a culture that supports the organisation's purpose and strategy
- The board defines and models a desired culture that aligns with the purpose and strategy
- The board oversees a strategy to develop and maintain the desired culture
- The board oversees mechanisms to monitor and evaluate organisational culture
- The organisation's values are clear, periodically reviewed and communicated to stakeholders
- The board oversees a framework for the reward and recognition of workers

While these principles make good sense, they are not enforceable. Other than the ACNC legislation, there is little else relating to governance and risk assurance practices in the NFP and charities sector. The sector does not face the same regulatory and market scrutiny as public companies, such as through capital markets. For example, only large charities and NFPs are required to be independently audited under the ACNC Act (medium-sized companies are only required to be reviewed). There are also no guidelines for measuring and reporting social outcomes or impacts.

Recent research has also shown that financial reporting requirements are not always consistently met by NFPs as they have discretion with respect to the financial reporting regime they apply (Yang and Simnett, 2020). For instance, large Australian charities that registered and lodged audited financial statements with the charities regulator on or after the reporting year 2014 (the first year of reporting to the ACNC) can choose from the following financial reporting frameworks: (1) general purpose financial statements following Australian Accounting Standards (GPFS-Tier 1); (2) general purpose financial statements following Australian Accounting Standards – Reduced Disclosure Requirements (GPFS-Tier 2); or (3) special purpose financial statements (SPFS), which involve a further reduced amount of disclosure in the financial statements (Yang and Simnett, 2020).

In fact, according to Yang and Simnett (2020), Australia is the only country in the world which allows NFPs to self-assess whether they will prepare GPFS or SPFS reports. Because it is possible for two similar charities to prepare very different financial statements, it is important to understand why some elect to follow a higher financial reporting standard than required.

Yang and Simnett's study (2020) found that 11,471 charities have consistent and reliable disclosure of their reporting framework, with just over half (55.68%) preparing GPFS and 44.32% preparing SPFS. Their further categorisation of GPFS found that 25.02% of charities prepare GPFS-Tier 1 reports, while 30.66% prepare GPFS-Tier 2 reports. Among the 2,473 charities appearing in the sample for all three years (the constant sample), the proportion reporting under GPFS-Tier 2 increased from 30.65% in 2014 to 35.99% in 2015, and to 37.85% in 2016. The authors suggest this shows a rapidly moving trend towards the reduced disclosure regime for GPFS reports.

Yang and Simnett's (2020) study also identified reporting risks and errors associated with a charity's disclosure of its financial reporting frameworks, as evidenced by many instances of either non-disclosure or discrepancies in the reporting framework identified by the charity and the framework identified by the auditor. As a result of their analysis, the Auditing and Assurance Standards Board (AUASB) immediately released a bulletin reiterating the auditor's responsibilities to evaluate whether financial statements adequately describe the applicable financial reporting framework as part of an auditor's work (Yang and Simnett, 2020) .

Ensuring high standards of governance

One way for market participants involved in an SII arrangement to ensure that service providers are meeting best practices for assurance and governance standards is to develop a checklist which addresses how well they are managing internal governance issues. This is considered particularly important given the strong links established in the literature between poor governance practices and bankruptcy risk (see Darrat et al., 2016).

A potential governance evaluation checklist could be developed using the Australian Institute of Company Directors' governance guidelines as a basis. Some key governance questions may include:

Organisational purpose and strategy

- Does the organisation prepare a corporate strategy?
- How frequently does the purpose and strategy get reviewed?
- Is the organisation's purpose and strategy clearly articulated and communicated to stakeholders?
- How effectively does the organisation's board align its decision-making with the strategy?

Financial statements and audit

- Are general purpose financial statements prepared by the organisation?
- Are the organisation's financial statements audited? By whom?
- Does the organisation comply with all applicable accounting standards?

Board roles and responsibilities

- Are the roles and responsibilities of the board and individual directors clear?
- Are any delegations of the board's authority clearly recorded and regularly reviewed?
- Is there an appropriate separation between the role of the board (governance) and of management (operations)?
- Are directors subject to any eligibility requirements and are they continuing to meet them?

Board composition

- Is the process for appointing directors clearly defined, transparent and followed?
- What is the board's current skills mix, and how is it communicated to stakeholders?
- Who will be leaving the board in the near-term future and is there a plan to respond?
- What skills will the board need in the future and how will they be accessed?

Board effectiveness

* How well prepared are new directors to take on their responsibilities?
* Do directors have access to the information they need to make informed decisions?
* Is there a tone of respect and collegiality in board meetings?
* Do directors understand the delineation between the roles of the board and management?
* What steps is the board taking, or should be taking, to improve its performance?

Risk management

* Is the board aware of how risk is managed in the organisation?
* Does the organisation have a risk management framework?
* How regularly is this framework reviewed?
* Is the framework aligned with the organisation's strategy?
* Does the board have access to external professional advice on risk management?

Performance

* Is the board satisfied that the organisation's resources are protected from misuse?
* Is there an agreed definition of success for this organisation?
* How well is financial and non-financial performance evaluated?
* Do financial performance targets contribute to long-term organisational sustainability?
* How does the board use performance information in its decision-making?

Accountability and transparency

* To whom is the organisation accountable?
* What information do stakeholders/members need to hold the board to account?
* How is reporting aligned with stakeholder/member needs?
* How can stakeholders/members hold the board to account for its decisions?
* What are the consequences for failing to meet stakeholder/member expectations?

Stakeholder engagement
* Who are the organisation's stakeholders?
* How are the needs of stakeholders considered by the organisation?

- How do stakeholders perceive the organisation and what is the impact of this?
- How does the board access and respond to feedback from stakeholders?
- How are vulnerable people protected by this organisation?

Conduct and compliance

- Are the behavioural expectations of the board clearly articulated?
- What are the consequences for failing to meet behavioural expectations?
- How effectively are conflicts of interest managed by the board?
- How does the board respond to bad news?
- What processes are in place to protect whistle-blowers?

Culture

- What sort of culture will best support the organisation to achieve its objectives?
- What is the culture of the organisation and how is this discerned?
- How often does the board discuss culture?
- How well does the behaviour of staff and volunteers align with the organisation's values?
- How does the board align its decision-making with its values?

Given the importance of the service provider to the overall success of any SII arrangement, we suggest the development of a 'best practice' assurance and governance framework for service providers. Investors and government are likely to place more confidence in service providers that have good corporate governance structures and rigorous assurance frameworks in place. Assurance involves the independent assessment of an organisation's governance arrangements, risk management and internal control processes. An effective assurance framework provides the connection between an organisation's strategic objectives (such as service delivery) and major risk factors which can undermine these objectives.

An effective assurance framework provides confidence to stakeholders in the SII market that the service provider's internal controls have been established and operate effectively to mitigate risk and that major operational and strategic challenges have been correctly identified and addressed.

Establishing a scoring model

This chapter has discussed a range of quantitative and qualitative factors for assessing the overall risk and performance of social service providers. It is possible to integrate these factors into a scoring model or rating system to assess the overall viability and performance of service providers. Rating systems are valuable because they condense complex information into unambiguous and objective measures or scores that can readily be interpreted by decision makers. Drawing on several themes discussed in this chapter, the framework in Table 6.1 is proposed for assessing and rating the overall risk and performance of a service provider.[6] In Table 6.1, we are considering a scenario where the social service provider is seeking private capital to fund a proposed social programme to be carried out by the service provider.

If each factor is rated on a 5-point Likert scale ranging from 1 (lowest score) to 5 (highest score), the final score can be tallied (the maximum score would be 5*11 = 55). More sophisticated could be added to the scoring approach by

TABLE 6.1 Framework for evaluating the viability and performance of social service providers

Risk and Performance Factor	Risk Direction (Positive, Neutral or Negative) and Score
Is there a pilot phase?	**Negative:** A pilot phase provides more assurance the social project can be successfully delivered. The absence of a pilot phase implies higher risk to the ultimate success of the project. **Score:**
Length of the project	**Positive:** The longer the duration of the social project, the higher the risk as there is potentially more time for extraneous factors or adverse circumstances to impact on the intervention. **Score:**
Track record of the service provider	**Negative:** More experienced service providers with proven track in social service delivery implies lower risk for service delivery. **Score:**
Quality of management	**Negative:** More experienced and appropriately qualified senior managers and service delivery teams reduce risk. **Score:**
Financial health	**Positive:** An adverse financial health rating (such as from any of the distress scoring models discussed above) clearly implies higher risk. Like any other organisation, social service providers require working capital and adequate revenue sources and cash flow to fund operations. If the intervention is being delivered over several years, it is important to monitor any changes in financial viability and performance. **Score:**

(continued)

TABLE 6.1 Cont.

Risk and Performance Factor	Risk Direction (Positive, Neutral or Negative) and Score
Financial disclosure and governance standards	**Negative:** Good financial disclosure and a strong set of governance standards suggest lower risk. Is the organisation detailed and transparent about corporate governance structures and financial disclosures? **Score:**
Compliance with regulation	**Negative:** Full compliance with all relevant regulations reduces risk. **Score:**
Data collection and reporting systems to capture accurate and timely data	**Negative** Systems to capture accurate and timely data are essential for reporting on progress in service delivery and reduces risk. **Score:**
Measurement of social outcomes	**Negative:** Service providers that provide clear, achievable, measurable and assessable social outcomes pose lower risk to investors. **Score:**
Level of evidence used for impact evaluation	**Negative:** A robust evaluation framework that uses randomised control designs, where appropriate, implies lower risk for investors and greater assurance that the intervention has been successful. **Score:**
How effectively can the evidence of outcomes be independently evaluated?	**Negative:** An independent evaluation suggests that the outcome measurement framework is rigorous and can be replicated by independent parties. This implies lower risk and greater assurance that the intervention has been successful. **Score:**

introducing heuristic weightings for different factors. For instance, financial health might receive a higher weighting than whether there is a pilot phase for the social programme or intervention. This scoring approach can also identify any noticeable deficiencies in any of the factors above. Even if the service provider receives a high overall rating, the variability of the factor scores is also important to consider. Scoring very poorly on one or two items may be consequential even if the overall score is strong. While Table 6.1 considers the scenario of a service provider seeking private capital to fund a social programme (such as in an SIB arrangement), the framework can be readily adapted to other social impact investment scenarios, such as a bank deciding whether to extend a loan to a social enterprise, an investor deciding whether to invest in a social enterprise (either directly or through an SIB arrangement) or a government agency deciding whether to participate in an SIB arrangement or fund (or renew funding) a service provider to deliver a social programme.

Key points from Chapter 6

For the Australian SII market to grow and meet the Taskforce's vision of becoming a deep market with many participants, and on a large scale, SII needs experienced intermediaries who can facilitate and structure SII investments (such as SIB arrangements). SVA and Social Finance in the UK are good examples of how intermediaries operate in the SII market.

One way to attract social impact investors, increase liquidity and access and provide clear exit strategies is to promote a secondary market such as a social stock exchange.

There are some notable examples of social impact exchange platforms around the world which have been established to provide a marketplace for both primary and secondary transactions including investment information on potential investment opportunities.

Current social stock exchanges around the world include the SSX which opened in the UK in June 2013, the SVX which opened in Canada in September 2013 and the IIX which opened in Singapore in June 2013.

If secondary markets for SII are to be effective and build investor confidence, there must be high-quality regulation and oversight, including effective corporate governance and transparency comparable to listed public companies.

For public companies, there are a wide range of risk evaluation models which regulators, auditors, creditors and investors can use to assess risk and financial performance.

In the case of an SIB, government performance payments are linked to the achievement of social outcomes. One of the key risks for an investor is that the service provider (which might be a private company, an NGO or an NFP entity) fails to deliver on the agreed outcomes.

In an SIB arrangement, the government cannot completely eliminate risk (e.g. lost progress payments if the SII arrangement fails). There is also potential reputational damage for government if the SIB arrangement fails.

Robust risk evaluation tools are therefore needed to evaluate the viability, capacity and quality of service providers (and social enterprises more broadly).

While most distress prediction models in the literature have been applied to publicly listed companies, many can be readily adapted to private companies, NGOs and NFP entities responsible for social service delivery.

In the financial distress literature, a variety of quantitative and qualitative frameworks have been utilised. Examples of risk models include simple probability models such as logit and probit models and advanced probability models such as mixed logit model, NL and latent class models.

More recently, artificial intelligence and machine learning models have been used to predict distress and bankruptcy and have ready applications to private company, NGO and NFP service providers.

Service providers also need effective and transparent assurance and governance frameworks to build and maintain investor confidence in the SII market. Charities and NFP entities are not necessarily subject to the same robust oversight and monitoring rules as listed public companies.

While the governance requirements of the ACNC Act 2012 are fairly minimal, the Australian Institute of Company Directors have set out ten more detailed governance principles for directors of charities and NFP entities: (1) purpose and strategy, (2) roles and responsibilities, (3) board composition, (4) board effectiveness, (5) risk management, (6) performance, (7) accountability and transparency, (8) shareholder engagement, (9) conduct and compliance and (10) culture.

One way for market participants involved in an SII arrangement to ensure that service providers are meeting best practices for assurance and governance standards is to develop a checklist which addresses how well they are managing assurance and governance risks. This is considered particularly important given the strong links established in the literature between poor governance practices and distress risk.

An effective assurance framework provides confidence to market participants in the SII market that the service provider's internal controls have been established and operate effectively to mitigate risk and that major operational and strategic challenges have been correctly identified and addressed.

There are a range of quantitative and qualitative factors for assessing the overall risk and performance of the service provider. It is possible to integrate these factors into a scoring model or rating system to assess current SII proposals or renewals for existing projects.

Drawing on several themes from this chapter, we propose a framework for rating the overall viability, performance and service delivery capacity of social service providers.

Notes

1 SVA has been involved in several SIB transactions across four states in Australia, including Newpin SA Social Impact Bond, Foyer Social Impact Bond, Side by Side Social Impact Bond, Sticking Together Social Impact Bond, Newpin Social Benefit Bond, Aspire Social Impact Bond, Resolve Social Benefit Bond and the Newpin Queensland Social Benefit Bond. SVA also provides debt and equity finance to social enterprises with positive social impact and capacity building services such as the SVA 'Upscaler' service. For more details, see SVA website: www.socialventures.com.au/impact-investing/our-social-impact-bonds (viewed 10 July 2021).

2 According to Jones and Hensher (2007), LCM is also free from many limiting statistical assumptions (such as linearity and homogeneity in variances) but avoids some of the analytical complexity of mixed logit.

3 These models are particularly powerful for handling a large number of predictor variables including variables of different types (such as continuous and categorical variables). Machine learning models have also been demonstrated to have stronger predictive power

than conventional statistical learning models. The general idea behind boosting is set out in the work of Schapire and Freund (2012).

4 Jones and Wang (2019) used the six classifications of private company failure adopted by Bureau van Dyke's ORBIS database which is one of the largest private company databases available containing over five million private companies. The ORBIS failure classifications include (1) default of payment, (2) firms subject to insolvency proceedings, (3) firms subject to bankruptcy proceedings, (4) firms which are dissolved (through bankruptcy), (5) firms in liquidation and (6) inactive firms (no precision). A major objective of Jones and Wang's (2019) study was to examine whether an advanced machine learning technique such as gradient boosting machines could be effective in predicting private company failure in multi-class settings. The key finding of Jones and Wang's (2019) is that machine learning predicts private company failure with a high degree of accuracy and significantly outperforms many of the conventional models discussed above.

5 See Australian Institute of Company Directors (2019, pp. 4–8).

6 Several organisations now provide some type of scoring model. For instance, SVA uses a scoring tool based on a series of questions relating to the following three themes: (1) the degree to which the organisation is client centred; (2) how effectively organisation is run in terms of planning, delivering, learning and governing; and (3) how the organisation engages with the ecosystem. The SVA impact assessment tool can be accessed at www.socialventures.com.au/learning-insights/sva-fundamentals-impact and providing registration details for downloading (viewed 10 July 2021).

7

APPROACHES TO MEASURING AND EVALUATING SOCIAL IMPACT

Introduction

This chapter considers social impact measurement and evaluation issues. We argue that social impact measurement is one of the most critical elements underpinning the operation of a successful social impact investing (SII) market. Without robust impact measurement, investors will not have a reliable basis for assessing the risk–return–impact trade-off, and impact measurement can easily fall prey to 'impact washing' (for example, where service providers can cherry pick their social impact metrics). While we are still some way off achieving generally accepted standards for the measurement, reporting and evaluation of social impact, a significant amount of work has been done globally. This chapter explores several international initiatives to measure and rate social impact from various networks and organisations, including B Lab and GIIRS rating system, the initiatives of the Global Impact Investing Network (GIIN), the Social Accounting Standards Board's (SASB) framework, the Global Reporting Initiative (GRI), the Impact Weighted Accounts (IWA) initiative, the United Nations (UN)'s Sustainable Development Goals (SDG), the iPAR Impact Framework, the Impact Management Project (IMP) and other approaches. This chapter also considers the importance of rigorous social impact evaluation in SII arrangements such as a social impact bond (SIB). We suggest that empirical evidence is required to show whether a social intervention has been successful or not with a high degree of reliability and confidence. Hence, the impact of a social programme or intervention needs to be isolated or 'controlled' for from other possible influences using sound methodologies, such as randomised control trials (RCTs). Chapter 7 also discusses some of the literature on how social impact evaluations are being implemented in practice.

DOI: 10.4324/9781003225591-7

Measuring social impact

Measuring social impact is one of the most critical elements underpinning a successful SII market. As stated in the Organisation for Economic Co-operation and Development (OECD) report 'Social Impact Investment 2019: The Impact Imperative for Sustainable Development' (p. 7):

> In order to harness the full potential of finance for sustainable development, we can't shy away from the urgent need for what this report calls 'the impact imperative': a shared understanding of how we measure the impact of our collective investments in sustainable development.

To use an accounting analogy, measuring impact has the same significance as measuring profitability for a corporation – without knowing its profitability, there is no way to gauge a company's growth, success or survival. In accounting practice, profits are measured using generally accepted accounting principles (GAAP) – a common set of accounting principles, standards and procedures issued by accountants to measure corporate profits and financial position. Without these principles, the measurement of corporate profit would be inconsistent across firms and could easily be subjected to income manipulation practices which could ultimately undermine the reliability and credibility of corporate earnings numbers.

The same can be said of impact measurement. Without robust impact measurement, investors will not have a reliable basis for assessing the risk–return–impact trade-off, and impact measurement can easily become prone to 'impact washing' (a concept similar to greenwashing discussed in Chapter 2). As stated by Cohen (2020, p. 30):

> A major benefit of impact measurement is that it presents the moral hazard of 'impact washing', when a business falsely claims to engage in socially beneficial work. For some businesses today, such claims are little more than a marketing ploy. In order to authentically integrate impact into business and investment decision-making, impact must be dependably measured.

The need for consistent and transparent impact metrics is further highlighted by Trelstad (2016b, p. 11):

> Finally, we must face the complex problem of measurability. There are still very few conventions on what evidence is sufficient to demonstrate proof of impact at the company level, how to aggregate that information at the fund level, and whether and how the sources of capital can evaluate the evidence to make rational investment decisions on the basis of an investment's combined financial and social or environmental returns. Everyone along the chain has an incentive and an ability to spin the story their way. In my

experience, many funds and the companies they invest in are attacking this problem with vigour and integrity. But at its heart, this is a collective action problem that can only be solved if funds and companies use standard impact accounting practices and consistent and transparent metrics, and are open to some type of independent verification, not unlike having a third party audit financial performance.

For impact investors to achieve the impact they intend to, advisors, fund managers, and the underlying companies in which they invest need to find ways to remain faithful to the investor's intent around impact. As it stands now, absent meaningful measures of social impact and incentives to achieve them, there is little to require anyone to comply with an investor's impact objectives beyond the minimum. This is not to say that all impact investments need to deliver the impact promised; all investments carry a risk of poor financial return. But without a mechanism to align all players in the impact value chain around an investor's expectations, the field risks an impact 'race to the bottom' where funds or companies do as little as possible to comply with an investor's objectives.

As stated in the OECD report (2019, p. 7), market regulators have an important responsibility in establishing appropriate impact measurement standards:

> Evidence presented in this report shows that, today, most investors seek market rate returns, and the assessment of achieved social outcomes is uneven at best. To counter the danger of 'impact washing', public authorities have the ultimate responsibility – in their capacity as market regulators, policy makers and development finance providers – to establish and promote integrity standards.

Given the challenges confronting the measurement of social outcomes (see, for example, Fox and Morris, 2021), we are still some way off in achieving generally accepted standards for the measurement, reporting and evaluation of social impact. However, on a more optimistic note, there has been a significant amount of work done internationally in terms of establishing guidelines and approaches for assessing impact performance across business organisations. For instance, according to the GIIN (2020a, p. 8) impact investor survey, there is evidence of a high reliance (89%) on external impact measurement systems, tools and frameworks. The survey indicates that the most commonly used resources are the SDGs (73%), the IRIS Catalog of Metrics (46%), IRIS+ Core Metrics Sets (36%) and the IMP's five dimensions of impact convention (32%) (see pp. 8–9).

In the following sections, we provide a brief review of different measurement and reporting frameworks used for impact investing around the world.

B Lab

B Lab is a not-for-profit entity founded in 2006 by the Rockefeller Foundation. B Lab has developed a comprehensive rating system known as the Global Impact

Investment Rating System (GIIRS) which can rate corporations and funds on their social and environmental impact (B Lab, 2020a). B Lab administers the B Corp Certification (where B stands for 'beneficial'). B Corp Certification identifies companies with exceptional positive social and environmental impact. B Corps certified companies must meet rigorous standards of verified performance, transparency and accountability (B Lab, 2020b).

B Corp Certification is based on the B Impact Assessment. All B Corps must measure their impact and achieve at least 80 points on the B Impact Assessment to gain certification. According to B Lab, any score above zero points is a 'good' score as it suggests the company is contributing something positive in terms of social impact. Each point earned above zero indicates incremental and positive impact. According to B Lab, most companies score between 40 and 100 points out of a possible 200 points (B Lab, 2020b).

Points are based on answers to questions, and the weightings of each question depend upon the specific 'assessment track'. The assessment track is determined by the industry, size and geography of the organisation being assessed. According to B Lab, points are received for every positive answer to a question and points are never lost. The questions cover the impact of a business on all stakeholders such as workers, suppliers, customers, community and the environment. The assessment is also designed to capture best practices regarding mission, measurement and governance (B Lab, 2020b).

The most heavily weighted portion of the assessment task identifies the company's specific 'impact business models' (i.e. the way the business seeks to have impact), which include the targeted, formal focus on benefiting a particular stakeholder through products and services or internal practices. For instance, a mining company would have more environmental impact than a retailer. Hence, more questions would be directed at environmental policies, practices and impact, and this would receive more weighting in the overall assessment (B Lab, 2020b).

The B Impact Assessment provides a judgement based on the scoring of how significant the social impact of the business is. B Corp Certification claims to go beyond the product or service level and measures a company's overall social and environmental performance. Certification is supported by transparency and accountability objectives that require businesses to consider long-term stakeholder by embedding it in their legal structure (B Lab, 2020b). Once certified, companies pay annual certification fees depending on their size. Currently, there are more than 1,700 B Corporations across 50 countries. However, most B Corporations tend to be small- and medium-sized private companies.

The Global Impact Investment Network (GIIN)

The GIIN is a not-for-profit organisation which refers to itself as a 'global champion of impact investing and dedicated to increasing its scale and effectiveness around the world' (GIIN, 2020c, para. 1). The GIIN has developed the Impact Reporting Investment Standard (IRIS) which provides a common reporting language to describe social and environmental performance to facilitate uniform and comparable measurement of impact across companies. The obvious advantage of this standardised approach is that it enables more consistent impact reporting and improved information for benchmarking.

IRIS+ are foundational materials that set out the core concepts and objectives that guide the GIIN in its approach to setting standards for impact measurement and management. Individual IRIS metrics are numerical measures used in calculations or qualitative values to account for the social, environmental and financial performance of an investment. The IRIS+ system references standard metrics and practices already in use by impact investors, from more than 50 entities. According to the GIIN (2020d, para. 1):

> IRIS+ is the generally accepted impact accounting system that leading impact investors use to measure, manage, and optimize their impact. Proper use of the IRIS+ system ensures a minimum level of consistency in a users' impact claims and performance, which makes it easier for investors to analyze and extract useful information for decision making. Use of IRIS+ also facilitates the comparison of impact information.

What distinguishes the IRIS+ system is its focus on contextualised evidence-based information on a range of impact themes or SDGs to help investors translate their impact intentions to results and make performance comparisons to ultimately optimise these results.

Sustainability Accounting Standards Board (SASB)

The SASB is a not-for-profit organisation founded in 2011 with the stated mission 'to establish industry-specific disclosure standards across ESG topics that facilitate communication between companies and investors about financially material, decision-useful information. Such information should be relevant, reliable and comparable across companies on a global basis' (2020a, para. 1).

To date, the SASB has developed a set of 77 industry-specific sustainability standards which identify the minimal set of 'financially material' sustainability topics and related metrics for the typical company in an industry. According to the SASB (2020b, para. 1), the focus on financially material issues is 'because our mission is to help businesses around the world report on the sustainability topics that matter most to their investors'. The SASB acknowledges that there is much environmental, social and governance (ESG) and sustainability information in the public domain. However, where it attempts to make a difference to investors is in identifying which ESG risk factors are most likely to impact the financial condition and operating performance of a company and affect investor decision-making.

The SASB provides a 'materiality map' (2020c) which identifies important sustainability themes likely to impact company performance. SASB outlines 26 sustainability-related business issues which encompass a range of disclosure topics and related accounting metrics. For example, the general issue category of customer welfare encompasses both the health and nutrition topic in the processed foods industry and the counterfeit drugs topic in the health-care distributors industry.

The 5 general categories and 26 sustainability topics covered by SASB (2020c, para. 2) are:

1. *Environment* which includes GHG emissions, air quality energy management, water and wastewater management, waste and hazardous materials management, ecological impacts.
2. *Social capital* which includes human rights and community relations, customer privacy, data security, access and affordability, product quality and safety, customer welfare, selling practices and product labelling
3. *Human capital* which includes labour practices, employee health and safety, employee engagement, diversity, and inclusion
4. *Business model and innovation* which includes product design and lifecycle management, business model resilience, supply chain management, materials sourcing and efficiency, physical impacts and climate change
5. *Leadership and governance* which includes business ethics, competitive behavior, management of the legal and regulatory environment, critical incident risk management and systemic risk management.

SASB standards are intended for voluntary use in disclosures required by existing US regulation in filings with the Securities and Exchange Commission (SEC), such as Forms 10-K and 20-F. Currently, around 120 companies are using SASB in their ESG reporting, and around 44 of these are international. Early adopters of SASB in the US that use the standards to report on material ESG issues include GM, Merck, Nike and JetBlue. According to the SASB, 72% of public companies make use of some industry-specific recommendations, while 28% make use of all of them (IR Magazine, 2019, para. 6). The majority of companies using the SASB framework also include it in their sustainability reports.

Global Reporting Initiative (GRI)

The GRI was founded in 1997 as a response to calls for greater corporate transparency resulting from the environmental damage caused by the Exxon Valdez oil spill.[1] It is an independent international organisation that 'helps businesses and other organizations take responsibility for their impacts, by providing them with the global common language to communicate those impacts'. According to its mission, the aim of the GRI 'was to create the first accountability mechanism to ensure companies adhere to responsible environmental conduct principles, which was then broadened to include social, economic and governance issues'.[2]

The first version of the GRI guidelines (G1) was published in 2000. G1 provided the first global framework for sustainability reporting. As demand for GRI reporting and uptake from organisations steadily grew, the guidelines were expanded and improved, leading to G2 (2001), G3 (2006) and G4 (2013). In 2016,

GRI transitioned from providing guidelines to setting the first global standards for sustainability reporting.[3] The Global Sustainability Standards Board (GSSB) has sole responsibility for setting the world's first globally accepted standards for sustainability reporting – the GRI Standards. Established as an independent operating entity under the auspices of GRI, GSSB members represent a range of expertise and multi-stakeholder perspectives on sustainability reporting. The GSSB claims to work exclusively in the public interest and according to the vision and mission of GRI. It sets out a new work programme every three years. The work programme includes projects to review existing GRI Standards as well as to develop new standards. In 2021, the GRI and SASB jointly published 'A Practical Guide to Sustainability Reporting Using GRI and SASB Standards'. This Guide provides key differences in GRI and SASB approaches and how each approach complements the other.

The Guide states (p. 5):

> GRI and SASB provide compatible standards for such disclosures. Their standards are mutually supportive and designed to fulfill different purposes. SASB's industry-specific standards identify the sustainability-related risks and opportunities most likely to affect a company's financial condition (i.e. its balance sheet), operating performance (i.e. its income statement), or risk profile (i.e. cost of capital). All of these factors impact a company's current and future market valuation. The GRI Standards focus on the economic, environmental and social impacts of the activities of a company, and hence its contributions – positive or negative – towards sustainable development. It is the underlying assumption that if not already financially material at the time of reporting, these impacts may become financially material over time. The GRI Standards support broad and comprehensive disclosures by providing the framework and supporting standards for a comprehensive understanding of the organization's impacts on economy, environment, and society including financially material impacts. SASB's Standards offer an industry-focused perspective by identifying the subset of issues that are reasonably likely to be financially material for the typical company in an industry. Each set of standards, therefore, complement rather than act as a substitute one another.

Based on a survey of 132 sustainability reporting organisations, the Guide (2021, p. 37) identified a number of benefits and challenges with using GRI standards and SASB standards in conjunction with each other.

Benefits

- They are both widely recognised high-quality reporting standards.
- They provide a common framework resulting in a comparable and consistent dataset for benchmarking and analysis.

- Disclosures meet the needs of a broad range of key stakeholders, supporting increased stakeholder engagement and improved disclosure for key audiences.
- Investors are catered for specifically.
- Reporting covers impacts *by* and impacts *on* the organisation.
- Reporting allows a gap analysis and comparison of reported issues and benchmark within or across sectors.
- Reporting provides alignment of materiality and support for materiality assessment.
- Easy and user-friendly frameworks.
- Covering bases: broad and sector-specific coverage.
- Possible to use with SDGs and other frameworks.
- Balance of social conscience and financial performance.

Challenges

- Balancing relevance and comprehensiveness of data.
- It is difficult to assess the usefulness of data that is asked for by stakeholders that are not investors.
- Divergent approach to materiality is the biggest issue, preferring to do only one materiality assessment to meet the needs of all stakeholders.
- Slight differences in metrics – e.g. SASB wants energy usage info in GJ, GRI in MWh; water volumes: GRI in megalitres, SASB in meters squared.
- Developing a report that is interesting and informative to all stakeholders while meeting the disclosure requirements of the standards.
- Complex (GRI) vs simple (SASB) – the Goldilocks effect.
- Lack of actionable linkages between the standards.
- Communicating benefit of using both internally and justifying the costs involved.
- Determining which SASB standards are most relevant.
- Time investment for mapping.
- ESG reporting moving faster than financial.
- How to make more quantitative and therefore comparable?

Impact-Weighted Accounts (IWA)

Accounting elements of the financial statements, such as assets, liabilities, equity, revenues and expenses are all measured and reported in financial statements in monetary terms or dollar amounts. Accounting conventions and GAAP which govern how financial statements are prepared also stress the importance of reliability and verifiability. For instance, verifiability is defined in the Australian conceptual framework for financial reporting (AASB, 2018, p. 16) as follows:

> Verifiability helps assure users that information faithfully represents the economic phenomena it purports to represent. Verifiability means that different

knowledgeable and independent observers could reach consensus, although not necessarily complete agreement, that a particular depiction is a faithful representation. Quantified information need not be a single point estimate to be verifiable. A range of possible amounts and the related probabilities can also be verified.

Generally, corporate financial statements do not report social and environmental impacts because they cannot be readily quantified or verified in monetary terms with sufficient reliability. A corporation can also have many possible social and environmental impacts, both positive and negative. It can be immensely challenging trying to decide which impacts to include, which are the most relevant, and to whom, and how they should be measured.

Despite these difficulties, the IWA project of Harvard University is challenging these core accounting assumptions and aims to produce financial statements which can capture a company's financial, social and environmental performance. Key principles driving the IWA project include (1) impact can be measured and compared; (2) impact should be measured within an accounting framework with the aim of harnessing our economy to improve our society and planet; (3) transformational change requires that impact measurement be scalable; and (4) to be scalable, it needs to be actionable and cost-effective.[4]

While challenging, it makes good sense to integrate social and environmental impacts formally into an accounting system. Frost et al. (2013) showed that when sustainability information was excluded from the accounting process and not subjected to rigorous measurement, organisations tended to ignore the information for most forms of internal decision-making, particularly financial decisions. Corporate managers and external users of the financial statements tended to concentrate heavily on financial metrics such as earnings per share. However, the overriding challenge is how to measure and integrate social and environmental information effectively so that the information has an acceptable level of reliability comparable to financial information.

As stated by Serafeim et al. (2019, p. 5):

> Impact-weighted accounts are line items on a financial statement, such as an income statement or a balance sheet, which are added to supplement the statement of financial health and performance by reflecting a company's positive and negative impacts on employees, customers, the environment and the broader society. The aspiration is an integrated view of performance which allows investors and managers to make informed decisions based not only on monetized private gains or losses, but also on the broader impact a company has on society and the environment.

An example of how to monetise social and environmental impact is provided by Freiberg et al. (2020). In this study, the authors develop a methodology for monetising environmental impact estimates 'by applying characterization pathways and monetization factors to organization level environmental outputs, including carbon emissions, water use, and other emission types' (2020, p. 1). The authors calculate environmental impact as a percentage of an organisation's sales and operating income, which they refer to as their 'environmental intensity' measure.

Across their sample, they find that the median environmental intensity to sales is 2% and the median environmental intensity to operating revenue is 20%. For 11 of the 67 industries in their sample, they find environmental intensity to sales is above 10% and environmental intensity to operating income is above 100%. They suggest this finding indicates a significant level of 'hidden liabilities' and potential for value erosion if environmental impacts are not correctly priced. Freiberg et al. (2020) also find that environmental intensity is statistically associated with lower corporate market valuation, lower stock returns and higher risk. This is consistent with investors viewing environmental impacts as being value relevant, financially impactful and important in corporate valuation.

The IWA project team have found 56 companies which have experimented with monetary impact valuation, producing environmental or total profit and loss accounts. Of these, 86% are estimating environmental impacts, 50% are estimating employment/social impacts and 20% are estimating product impacts. The IWA project notes there is broad representation across Global Industry Classification Standard (GICS) Industry Sectors; however, the material sector was represented the most with 12 companies performing monetary valuation, most from the chemical industry.

Sustainable Development Goals (SDGs)

According to the UN (2020, para.1), the SDGs are:

> A universal call to action to end poverty, protect the planet and improve the lives and prospects of everyone, everywhere. The 17 Goals were adopted by all UN Member States in 2015, as part of the 2030 Agenda for Sustainable Development which set out a 15-year plan to achieve the Goals.

The 17 SDGs are (1) no poverty; (2) zero hunger; (3) good health and well-being; (4) quality education; (5) gender equality; (6) clean water and sanitation; (7) affordable and clean energy; (8) decent work and economic growth; (9) industry, innovation and infrastructure, (10) reducing inequality; (11) sustainable cities and communities; (12) responsible consumption and production; (13) climate action; (14) life below water; (15) life on land; (16) peace, justice, and strong institutions; and (17) partnerships for the goals.

Though the SDGs are broad and interdependent, two years later (6 July 2017), they were made more 'actionable' by a UN Resolution adopted by the General Assembly. The resolution identifies specific targets for each goal together with indicators to measure progress towards each target. Each target is usually intended to be achieved between 2020 and 2030. For some of the targets, no end date is given. A variety of tools have been developed to monitor, track and visualise progress towards the goals and are intended to make data more available and easily understood. For example, the online publication SDG-Tracker, launched in June 2018, presents available data across all indicators. The SDGs pay attention to multiple cross-cutting issues, for example, gender equality, education and culture cut across all of the SDGs.

Sources of funding for the SDGs are a continuing concern. The Rockefeller Foundation hosted a workshop (June 2017: Scaling Solutions) and concluded that 'while there is a moral imperative to achieve the SDGs, failure is inevitable if there aren't drastic changes to how we go about financing large scale change'.

iPAR Impact

iPAR Impact is a tool launched in April 2016 which allows impact investors to compare social and environmental impact across their portfolios. iPAR claims to facilitate better reporting and more intuitive analysis of impact investing. According to iPAR (2020a, para. 1), metrics today fail to properly inform investors for several reasons:

1. *Too esoteric/specific:* litany of minutia-filled metrics defies concise communication and easy interpretation.
2. *Devoid of necessary context:* some investors don't understand what is being tracked or why.
3. *Indiscernible significance:* some managers report metrics that aren't tied to their impact strategy success.
4. *Missing target/goals:* results oftentimes exist in a vacuum, with no way to ascertain performance.

The iPAR framework (iPAR, 2020b) recognises that there is currently no standardised way to classify impact intent or geographic focus. Categorisation supports recognition, differentiation and comprehension – three characteristics that are essential for new investors entering the ecosystem. For investors, iPAR accelerates identification of mission-aligned strategies. For managers, iPAR promotes clarification of impact intentions. An iPAR profile disaggregates every manager's impact intentions into the most important components (referred to as 'building blocks'). Each of the building blocks is then evaluated separately from their financial return expectations – facilitating comparison of dissimilar investment. The risks to impact creation are also distilled into a quantifiable figure. This assessment creates a baseline against which future progress can be evaluated. Impact metrics are designed to foster two-way communication between impact managers and investors, contextualise each impact metric, illuminate historic performance to see accumulation of impact over time and codify manager expectations and targets to facilitate improved analysis.

Impact Management Project (IMP)

The IMP (2020a, 2020b) provides a forum for over 2,000 organisations (i.e. the Practitioner Community) to build global consensus on how to define, manage, measure, assess and report impacts on environmental and social issues. IMP provides a forum for businesses and investors committed to managing ESG risks as well as contributing to positive goals. This consensus (or 'norms') provide a common logic to help enterprises and investors understand their impacts on people and the planet in order to reduce the negative and increase the positive (IMP, 2020b). Impact is defined as 'a change in an outcome caused by an organisation. An impact can be positive or negative, intended or unintended' (2020b, para. 3). The IMP (2020b, para. 10) reached global consensus that impact can be measured across five dimensions:

1. '*What*' tells us what outcome the enterprise is contributing to, whether it is positive or negative, and how important the outcome is to stakeholders?
2. '*Who*' tells us which stakeholders are experiencing the outcome and how underserved they are in relation to the outcome?
3. '*How much*' tells us how many stakeholders experienced the outcome, what degree of change they experienced and how long they experienced the outcome for.
4. '*Contribution*' tells us whether an enterprise's and/or investor's efforts resulted in outcomes that were likely better than what would have occurred otherwise.
5. '*Risk*' tells us the likelihood that impact will be different than expected.

Social Value International (SVI)

The Social Return on Investment (SROI) Network (now Social Value UK) and Social Impact Analysts Association joined forces to create SVI which advocated the use of SROI. This is a ratio that reflects the dollar social value created for every dollar of investment. This is an outcome-based metric that helps businesses to monetise and quantify the amount of social, environmental and economic value they are creating. An SROI analysis indicates how a business creates and destroys value in the course of its operations and activities.

SVI's Principles of Social Value (2020, para. 9) are stated as follows:

1. *Involve stakeholders* – inform what gets measured and how this is measured and valued in an account of social value by involving stakeholders.
2. *Understand what changes* – articulate how change is created and evaluate this through evidence gathered, recognising positive and negative changes as well as those that are intended and unintended.
3. *Value the things that matter* – making decisions about allocating resources between different options needs to recognise the values of stakeholders. Value refers to the relative importance of different outcomes. It is informed by stakeholders' preferences.

4. *Only include what is material* – determine what information and evidence must be included in the accounts to give a true and fair picture, such that stakeholders can draw reasonable conclusions about impact.
5. *Do not over-claim* – only claim the value that activities are responsible for creating.
6. *Be transparent* – demonstrate the basis on which the analysis may be considered accurate and honest and show that it will be reported to and discussed with stakeholders.
7. *Verify the result* – ensure appropriate independent.

How does SROI fit with these principles? According to SVI, SROI is a framework which applies all of the principles above to account for social value, with the added condition that Principle 3: 'Value the things that matter' is achieved through the use of financial proxies. SROI is an account of value creation which uses a mix of qualitative, quantitative and financial information. Social Value UK (2012, pp. 6–7) contextualise the rationale for using SROI as follows:

> There is increasing recognition that we need better ways to account for the social, economic and environmental value that results from our activities. The language varies – 'impact', 'returns', 'benefit', 'value' – but the questions around what sort of difference and how much of a difference we are making are the same. Understanding and managing this broader value is becoming increasingly important for the public and private sectors alike. This is true whether it is civil society organisations working to create value, Governments commissioning and investing in activities to create social value, investors seeking to ensure that their investments will make a difference, or private businesses recognising both risk and opportunity in the wider effects of operations. All this means that it is also more important that we have some consistency and a shared language when we talk about value. SROI is the application of a set of principles within a framework that is designed to help bring about that consistency, whilst at the same time recognising that what is of value will be very different for different people in different situations and cultures.

Calculating SROI

Social Value UK (2012, pp. 16–78) also outlines six stages for carrying out an SROI analysis:

1. Establishing scope and identifying key stakeholders. The SVI advises that it is important to have clear boundaries about what the SROI analysis will cover, who will be involved in the process, and how.
2. Mapping outcomes. This stage involves engaging with stakeholders to develop an impact map, or theory of change, which shows the relationship between inputs, outputs and outcomes.

3. Evidencing outcomes and giving them a value. This stage involves finding data to show whether outcomes have happened and then valuing them.
4. Establishing impact. Having collected evidence on outcomes and monetised them, those aspects of change that would have happened anyway or are a result of other factors are eliminated from consideration.
5. Calculating the SROI. This stage involves adding up all the benefits, subtracting any negatives and comparing the result to the investment. This is also where the sensitivity of the results can be tested.
6. Reporting, using and embedding. SVI advise this vital last stage involves sharing findings with stakeholders, embedding good outcomes processes and verification of the report.

The advantage of SROI is that social impact is included in return on investment which provides a more holistic interpretation of business performance that extends beyond traditional financial measures. The fact that SROI is monetised can help decision makers make more informed economic decisions. The SROI process is also participative and includes stakeholder groups which can help businesses better understand how their business activity is having impact. The limitation of SROI is that the analysis relies on high-quality impact data which is not always available. SROI is also a single ratio which is only useful when interpreted in the broader context of a company's activities. Hence, the ratio is not necessarily useful for comparative purposes.

Social Impact Measurement Network Australia (SIMNA)

SIMNA is a membership-based organisation whose objective is to help foster social impact measurement in Australia. The organisation was established following a three-year Investing in Impact Partnership (IIP), established by Social Ventures Australia, the Centre for Social Impact (CSI) and PwC from 2009 to 2012. In October 2011, a Social Impact Measurement in Australia conference was held and supported by IIP project partners. According to its website, SIMNA's activities to date have included the following:

- Member participation and networking around Australia as part of state chapters.
- Co-convening the Think Outcomes conference in Sydney (2014) and Melbourne (2016).
- Celebrating success in social impact measurement through the SIMNA Awards.

A review of social impact measurement approaches was provided by Shinwell and Shamir (2018). The authors reviewed 35 business frameworks and initiatives that purport to measure the impacts of business on people's well-being and sustainability from a variety of sources. These represent the leading initiatives in this field, such as the GRI and Sustainability Accounting Standards Board (SASB) and leading businesses reporting on ESG issues. They also identified several businesses that are leaders on reporting on the wider impacts of their operations and consulted with various experts from academia, the business sector and civil society organisations.

Shinwell and Shamir (2018, p. 34) conclude that:

> this review finds that the current landscape of the business impact measurement field is fragmented and insufficient. The proliferation of measurement frameworks is a burden on companies, which are pursuing alignment with multiple frameworks simultaneously, and for stakeholders, in terms of choosing which one to follow, and does not make business impact data comprehensible, comparable and actionable. Despite the progress made in this area over the past few decades, we are still far away from having achieved a good balance between companies' measuring and reporting burden and different stakeholders' demand for accurate information.

Shinwell and Shamir (2018, pp. 34–35) identify particular challenges to impact measurement, which is not surprising given the evolving nature of the field and the fact that that impact measurement and reporting is largely voluntary. Their findings included (1) measurement frameworks are not sufficiently detailed and transparent about metrics and methodologies (particularly ratings providers charging fees); (2) the structure and content of business annual reports, and sustainability indicators reported therein, vary significantly between different companies and from year to year, making it difficult to track performance over time; (3) high-quality and up-to-date data on business impacts feature in several reporting frameworks targeted at investors who are charged for these services, limiting accessibility and limit transparency of frameworks targeted at broader stakeholder groups; (4) industry-specific metrics are reported in many frameworks but can be a double-edged sword; (5) developing business-level SDGs measurement metrics for business is still a distant goal; (6) the exclusion of relevant information (including some business impacts while excluding others) can limit comparability across firms; (7) measurement inconsistencies (such as different measurement scales and units are prevalent across different frameworks); and (8) use of company-specific definitions and standards can undermine the consistency and comparability of information.

Because social impact measurement and reporting is voluntary, wide variations in practice and reporting inconsistencies across companies are to be expected. As recommended by the Global Social Impact Investment Steering Group (see Chapter 5) and Cohen (2020), one solution to address the issues above is for governments to implement mandatory impact measurement, auditing and reporting standards similar to those used in corporate financial reporting. A uniform approach to measurement, and further requirements to have impact disclosures independently audited, could significantly improve intra-company and intra-industry consistency and comparability of social impact disclosures provided by companies.

Evaluating social outcomes

Just as there needs to be rigorous measurement of social impact, there also need to be robust evaluation frameworks for determining how successful a social programme or intervention has been. How can we be sure that an intervention was effective? Was the intervention successful only by chance? Was the intervention only partly successful? What type of evidence needs to be presented to demonstrate the success of a programme?

If we want to show the intervention has been successful with a high degree of reliability and confidence, then empirical evidence is required, particularly if we wish to show the intervention is statistically and economically significant. Thus, the effect of the intervention must be isolated or 'controlled' for from other possible influences. For example, consider an initiative to help young offenders find a job through a mobile phone app designed to link them to potential employers. How would we assess the effectiveness of the intervention? If it is found that 30% managed to find jobs over the intervention period, would this be sufficient evidence to show the intervention was successful? Probably not.

It is possible that their job success had nothing to do with the app but coincided with a nationwide improvement in the employment levels over the intervention period or simply by chance (it would have happened anyway without the app). How can we be confident the intervention itself was effective? To take the guesswork out of it, we need to use experimental design methodologies and interpret the results using the rules of statistical inference.

To be more certain of the effect of the app, we need to design a pre-test and post-test experiment with a control group. Measurements need to be taken before the app was provided to the young offender sample. In other words, we need to know something about the success rate of young offenders finding employment before the app was introduced. We then need to compare this to the results after the intervention is administered. This is called the post-test measurement. The difference in the pre- and post-test measurements is the result of the experimental treatment or intervention.

If the pre-test measurement indicates a 10% success rate for finding jobs, and the post-measurement is 40%, the intervention has improved the success rate by 30% in absolute terms. While we would have more confidence in the results using a pre-test post-test design, we still cannot be certain whether the app actually caused the increase in employment. While it may seem very effective, the experiment does not control for extraneous or outside factors that may have influenced the results, such as a general improvement in the job market over this period or perhaps the introduction of new government employment programmes during the intervention.

There also needs to be a control group of job-seeking young offenders who did not have access to the app over the intervention period. If there are statistical differences in the ability of young offenders to find jobs both with and without the app after controlling for extraneous factors (such as the job market), we would then conclude the intervention was successful. However, we still need to keep in mind that statistical significance does not always equate to economic significance. A small improvement in employment might be statistically significant but not economically meaningful to justify the claim the intervention was impactful. Some discretion is required for interpreting the economic significance of the impact alongside the statistical significance of the experimental results.

The experiment also needs to be reliable. There needs to be a meaningful way to track whether the app was accessed for its intended use and actually measures what it purports to measure (job opportunities for young offenders).

Another factor to consider is the power of the statistical tests. For example, there may be statistically significant differences in the ability of the app to improve job prospects for young offenders, but if the experimental results are based on sample sizes that are too small, this will reduce the power of the tests and diminish confidence in the findings.

We also need to evaluate impact in terms of any negative effects of the impact. For instance, was using the app stressful or inconvenient to young offenders or did they end up finding jobs in undesirable occupations or locations?

It is also important to consider the standards of evidence used in practice for evaluating social outcomes. One example is provided by the Nesta Impact Investment fund. As can be seen from Table 7.1, Nesta provides a five-level framework for evaluating evidence of impact (Puttick & Ludlow, 2012). Level 1 simply entails providing a coherent account of the impact and expected outcomes. Level 2 is more demanding and involves some data collection to show some change resulting from the intervention. At this stage, evidence of causality is not required, but data collection could involve the use of surveys/interviews.

Level 3 goes further and requires some demonstration that the intervention is actually causing the impact (by showing less impact by those not subject to the intervention). At this stage, a randomised control group with adequate sample sizes would be required to demonstrate evidence. Level 4 requires an explanation of how and why the intervention had an observable impact. At this stage, independent evaluation of the impact and the ability to replicate the intervention in multiple locations is essential. Level 5 requires that the intervention can be operated and scaled up by someone else in other locations. This would require multiple replication evaluations, future scenario analysis and fidelity analysis.

Another example of impact evaluation used in practice is employed by the NSW Office of Social Impact Investment (OSII). The OSII (2018b, p. 11) uses a hierarchical evidence-based framework for assessing SII proposals based on the following principles:

- A proposal must clearly identify the target population of the intervention and describe the criteria to define the intervention group.
- The overall logic of how the intervention is expected to work (i.e. the program logic) needs to be clear and based on quantitative evidence of its effectiveness.
- The primary outcome measure must be objective, reliable and collectable, and be linked to the social and financial benefits of the intervention.

TABLE 7.1 Nesta output evaluation framework

Level	Our Expectation	How the Evidence Can Be Generated
At Level 1	You can give an account of impact. By this we mean providing a logical reason, or set of reasons, for why your products/service could have impact on one of our outcomes and why that would be an improvement on the current situation.	You should be able to do this yourself and draw upon existing data and research from other sources.
At Level 2	You are gathering data that shows some change among those using your product/service.	At this stage, data can begin to show effect, but it will not evidence direct causality. You could consider such methods as: pre- and post-survey evaluation, cohort/panel study and regular interval surveying.
At Level 3	You can demonstrate that your product/service is causing the impact, by showing less impact among those who don't receive the product/service.	We will consider robust methods using a control group (or another well-justified method) that begin to isolate the impact of the product/service. Random selection of participants strengthens your evidence at this level; you need to have a sufficiently large sample at hand (scale is important in this case).
At Level 4	You are able to explain why and how your product/service is having the impact you have observed and evidenced so far. An independent evaluation validates the impact you observe/generate. The product/service delivers impact at a reasonable cost, suggesting that it could be replicated and purchased in multiple locations.	At this stage, we are looking for a robust independent evaluation that investigates and validates the nature of the impact. This might include endorsement via commercial standards, industry Kitemarks, etc. You will need documented standardisation of delivery and processes. You will need data on costs of production and acceptable price point for your customers.
At Level 5	You can show that your product/service could be operated up by someone else, somewhere else and scaled up, while continuing to have positive and direct impact on the outcome and remaining a financially viable proposition.	We expect to see use of methods like multiple replication evaluations; future scenario analysis; fidelity evaluation.

Source: Puttick and Ludlow (2012, p. 8) (Nesta).

- Outcome definitions should specify with what, when and how outcomes will be measured.
- The sample size should ideally provide at least 80% power to detect the effect, if any, of the intervention.
- A randomised design is the most robust way of assessing an intervention's impact.
- When randomisation is not possible, every effort should be made to create a control group that is as similar as possible to the intervention group and collect information on potential confounding factors. Where a control group is not possible or appropriate in the circumstances, other counterfactuals such as a historical baseline should be explored.
- Proposals should also discuss data management and ethics implications.

According to the OSII (2018b, pp. 12–23), the robustness and quality of measurement largely depends on the design of the intervention to allow effective evaluation and relies on the four 'PICO' pillars (population, intervention, outcomes, counterfactual) as follows:

- *Population.* Social impact proposals should clearly identify the target population and how individuals will be selected to participate in the proposed intervention. OSII states that

  > if the definition of the target population is not focused enough, the intervention may be too diffuse to have a significant impact on the target outcome. If the definition is too narrow, the target population may not be large enough to require a dedicated service or be generalised to a wider group.
  >
  > *OSII, 2018b, p. 12*

- *Intervention.* Programme logic (or the visual representation of how an intervention works) is used to explain how an intervention works and why. It should provide a clear and credible account of impact, setting out why the intervention is expected to have a positive effect on the outcome. It should explain why the impact of the intervention is expected to go beyond what would have happened without it and why it is expected to improve outcomes compared to business as usual or competing interventions (if any).
- *Outcomes.* Measurement is at the heart of SII. Robust metrics are required to demonstrate to SII participants that impact objectives have been successfully achieved. Outcomes range from the ultimate outcome used to quantify the definitive impact of the intervention, to intermediate and process outcomes that quantify the fidelity of implementation.
- *Counterfactual.* The most important aspect in measuring the impact of an intervention is getting a reliable estimate of the counterfactual (i.e. an estimate of what would have happened in the absence of the intervention). OSII require impact proposals to consider how to assess whether social impacts can be

attributed to the intervention. The most important aspect of the counterfactual is that it constitutes a clear and quantifiable estimate of the impact of the intervention.

While randomised control designs are ultimately the most robust way to evaluate social impact, in practice they can be costly and time-consuming to implement, and in the case of social programmes, they are not always appropriate or possible. Hence, not all social impact investments will be evaluated by such robust criteria. As stated in Saltuk (2012, p. 42) 'A Portfolio Approach to Impact Investment: A Practical Guide to Building, Analysing and Managing a Portfolio of Impact Investments':

> Rigorous impact evaluation, including Randomized Control Trial ('RCT'), is powerful, but onerous and expensive in practice. Many impact investors therefore settle for measuring 'activities' or 'outputs' (such as number of bednets sold) rather than running control groups to measure the 'impact'. Investors balance the need for rigorous impact evaluation against the need for simple, cost effective ways of measuring this impact. We believe the tools being developed to balance these needs should build on knowledge generated by the existing body of academic literature, while acknowledging the need for systems that add value and are pragmatic for investment activity.

And further:

> There could also be ethical questions about running control groups if it meant denying the product or service to a part of the population that should have equal access.
>
> *Footnote 33, p. 42*

Fox and Morris' (2021) systematic review of evaluations of payment-by-results (PbR) and SIB programmes in the UK since 2010 found a dearth of impact evaluation practices, even for some very large PbR programmes.[5] Fox and Morris (2021) also found that the quality of impact evaluations is not particularly high (p. 69). For instance, most PbR evaluations were 'process evaluations' with very few impact evaluations provided (p. 65). O'Flynn and Barnett (2017) suggest, among other reasons, that the lack of rigorous impact evaluation could be due to (1) the cost of implementing external valuations of PbRs and SIBs, (2) the administrative burden external evaluations can put on service providers, (3) the fact that impact might be implicitly assumed in some programmes and hence does not or should not require a formal assessment and (4) the fact that social impacts can take some time to materialise after the initial impact investment. Fox and Morris (2021, p. 65) also suggest that the complexity of designing evaluations can also contribute to the lack of rigour. They argue this is 'often due to the difficulty of finding a comparator; and, debates about methodology within the evaluation sector that can be off-putting to commissioners'.[6] While Fox and Morris (2021, p. 69) advocate the use of RCTs, they also suggest improvements in relation to outcome-based evaluations (such as the incorporation of mixed-methods, more rigorous theories of social change and paying greater attention to context).

While the lofty academic standards for scientific evidence and discovery cannot always be achieved in the time poor world of practice, there can be serious risks with abandoning scientific evidence as basis for impact evaluation altogether. Relying on the measurement and evaluation of activities and outputs alone, while a compromise for some, can ultimately undermine the credibility of the SII market.

Key points from Chapter 7

Measuring social impact is a critical element underpinning a successful SII market. To use an accounting analogy, measuring impact has the same significance as measuring profitability for a corporation.

Without robust impact measurement, investors will not have a reliable basis for assessing the risk–return–impact trade-off, and impact measurement can easily result in 'impact washing'.

While we are still some way off in achieving generally accepted standards for the measurement, reporting and evaluation of social impact, a significant amount of work has been done globally.

B Lab has developed a comprehensive rating system known as the GIIRS which can rate corporations on their social and environmental impact. B Lab administers the B Corp Certification which identifies companies with exceptional positive social and environmental impact.

The GIIN has developed the IRIS which provides a common reporting language to describe social and environmental performance to facilitate uniform and comparable measurement of impact across companies.

If we seek to show the intervention has been successful with a high degree of reliability and confidence, then empirical evidence is required, particularly if we wish to show the intervention is statistically and economically significant. Hence, the effect of the intervention must be isolated or 'controlled' for from other possible influences using RCTs.

While robust evaluations using RCTs are common in the US and Australia, empirical research by Fox and Morris (2021) suggest they are less prevalent in the UK.

Notes

1 The history of the GRI is available on the GRI website: www.globalreporting.org/about-gri/mission-history (viewed 10 July 2021).
2 www.globalreporting.org/about-gri/mission-history (viewed 10 July 2021).
3 www.globalreporting.org/about-gri/mission-history (viewed 10 July 2021).
4 See the IWA website for more information. www.hbs.edu/impact-weighted-accounts/Pages/default.aspx (viewed 10 July 2021).

5 This seems to contrast with the US and Australia where randomised control designs are common in SIB evaluations.
6 Fox and Morris (2021, p. 66) conclude that the majority of PbR and SIB evaluations were 'reasonably strong' on issues such as data collection, analysis and reporting. However, they note consistent areas of weakness to include (1) absence of a theory of change; (2) sampling (i.e. rarely a clear rationale provided); (3) discussion of design or methodology; and (4) research ethics, addressed in only a minority of studies.

8

EPILOGUE AND FUTURE DIRECTIONS

This book has navigated the landscape of social impact investing (SII) both in Australia and internationally. While SII is a relatively new concept, the market has grown significantly over the past decade, and the momentum continues unabated. There is a powerful imperative behind SII to fundamentally reshape modern capitalism and harness the power of capital markets to address pressing social and environmental challenges such as lack of adequate education and healthcare, homelessness, refugee crises and climate change. A plethora of different networks and organisations, such as the Global Impact Investing Network (GIIN), Social Accounting Standards Board (SASB), Global Reporting Initiative (GRI) and B Lab, have emerged to champion the cause of SII and provide companies, fund managers and other users with robust frameworks and tools to better measure, report and evaluate on social impact. Various investor surveys sponsored by GIIN, JP Morgan and other organisations have revealed a strong appetite for impact investing across a wide cross section of global investors.

Notwithstanding that many early experimentations with social impact bonds (SIBs) and other SII arrangements have proven quite successful, it remains something of an anomaly that the actual amount of impact investment remains quite modest in global terms, particularly in Australia. While the Australian government appears to have embraced SII, actual SII investment remains quite negligible in this country.

What more can be done to facilitate the growth of the SII market in this country? The position taken in this book is that government needs to take a more significant and active role in developing and growing a robust and vibrant SII market. We believe there is much more the government can do as a market facilitator, a market regulator and as a market participant. There are numerous recommendations, strategies and proposals suggested by various Taskforce reports, government studies as well as academic- and practitioner-related literature. Some of the more useful recommendations in the Australian context include the following.

DOI: 10.4324/9781003225591-8

Facilitate creation of secondary markets for SII

The government can help establish a social stock exchange in Australia including sponsoring the creation of a social investment wholesaler similar to Big Society Capital in the UK. There are several examples of social stock exchange platforms around the world discussed in Chapter 6. We would suggest a similar social stock exchange to the SSX in London. While the SSX is not a regulated stock exchange, and is not involved in actual share trading, it has a rigorous three-stage process for admission including (1) the requirement to be admitted to a regulated stock exchange such as the London Stock Exchange; (2) the production of an Impact Report detailing how well the business has performed against key social performance targets; and (3) an assessment of social impact by the SSX's admissions panel, formed of leading SII experts.

Listing on a social stock exchange will facilitate more deal origination or deal sourcing as investors and social entrepreneurs come together to create a more vibrant and fluid environment for social impact investment.

The government could also support the establishment of a social investment institution such as Big Society Capital in the UK. Big Society Capital is an independent financial institution authorised and regulated by the Financial Conduct Authority (FCA). It acts as a social investment wholesaler to promote the development of the social investment marketplace in the UK. Big Society Capital sources its funds from two streams: English dormant bank account (invested via The Oversight Trust – Assets for the Common Good) and four major UK investment banks: Barclays, HSBC, Lloyds Banking Group and Natwest Group. Big Society Capital has been running quite successfully as investment wholesaler and as an active facilitator of the social investment market in the UK. Impact Investing Australia (2016) has proposed the establishment of a social investment wholesale very similar to Big Society Capital in its proposal 'Blueprint to Market: Impact Capital Australia'. The purpose of creating Impact Capital Australia is to provide more scale to the current Australian market to maximise opportunities to deliver positive social outcomes in this country. According to the 'Blueprint to Market', the wholesaler approach has particular benefits in creating a 'multiplier effect' – by investing in intermediaries who bring impact investments to market (who then invest in the front line of impact-driven organisations), the wholesaler can lever their investments by allowing intermediaries to do more with existing resources while increasing the flow of capital to the market. The proposal to create Impact Capital Australia is still awaiting government funding.

Mandating companies to measure and report on their social impact

As shown in Chapter 5, impact reporting standards affect all market participants, including those who demand impact capital, those who supply impact capital, intermediaries (who structure impact transactions for market participants or fund impact investments) and ecosystem enablers. A major theme of this book is that impact measurement and reporting is at the heart of a successful SII market. Mainstream capital markets operate with a high level of investor confidence which can be attributed, at least in part, to high-quality regulatory oversight over the operations of markets. Companies must legally comply with generally accepted accounting principles (GAAP) and international financial reporting standards in Australia including various auditing and assurance standards. Corporations must also comply with many other statutory regulations to ensure the efficient functioning and transparency of the market.

For a secondary market, such as a social stock exchange, to operate on an equal footing with mainstream capital markets, would require rigorous regulation of impact-driven enterprises in areas such as corporate governance, financial disclosure and auditing, generally agreed on concepts of impact measurement, and social outcome evaluation frameworks. At a minimum, private companies, non-government organisations (NGOs) and not-for-profit (NFP) entities engaged in social service delivery should be required to measure and report on their social impacts to stakeholders. If this becomes a legal requirement, standard setting bodies (such as the Financial Accounting Standards Board (FASB), SASB and GRI) will likely move more quickly to the develop standards and principles of best practice as we see in corporate financial reporting regulation.

Accounting standard setters generally avoid impact reporting (and corporate social responsibility [CSR] more generally) due to the difficult and seemingly intractable measurement problems. While there are many initiatives around the world to develop standards for impact measurement, these initiatives are all voluntary and principles based, ultimately reducing their effectiveness when companies try to apply them. A mandatory requirement for impact measurement and reporting could be a game changer in terms of accelerating general accepted principles for impact measurement, reporting and evaluation, particularly if standard setters take the lead on these issues. As a minimum, the government should facilitate a standardised impact reporting framework as well as encouraging the disclosure of non-financial information.

Government as a purchaser of social outcomes

As suggested by the Australian Taskforce report on Social Impact Investing and the G8 Social Impact Investing Taskforce report (2014), government can become a more proactive purchaser of social outcomes by promoting outcome-based contracting on a larger scale than it is presently. It can also support social enterprises through integrating social outcome objectives formally into procurement policy.

An effective way to purchase social outcomes is to support more SIB arrangements in Australia. As this book has illustrated, SIBs have significant potential to transform the SII market. SIBs can potentially benefit all market participants, including impact investors (who are seeking social impact alongside financial returns), service providers (who can receive capital upfront rather than when outcomes are achieved) and government who can potentially save taxpayer dollars through more innovative and cost-effective social service delivery mechanisms. A further benefit for government is that SIBs can transfer risk to private investors who will bear the full cost of a social programme if it fails. SIB arrangements are usually structured to require the measurement of social impact as well as having outcomes independently evaluated. This implies governments are likely to be purchasing social outcomes in more effective, transparent and better managed social projects. Another advantage of SIBs is that these can encourage more innovation and experimentation. Social programmes can be tailored to specific social objectives or priorities, such as preventive interventions or social issues currently unmet by government.

Improve quality of data on social issues

The view taken in this book is that more can be done in Australia to improve the quantity, quality and integration of social impact data, including interlinking large government databases to extract better quality data on the cost of social issues. This can inform SII participants and further the objectives of the SII market by improving the measurement, reporting and evaluation of social outcomes. The UK government, for instance, has developed initiatives such as the unit cost database which brings together more than 800 cost estimates into a single location. Most of which are national costs derived from government reports and academic studies (New Economy, 2015). The unit cost database covers the following social themes (a) crime, (b) education and skills, (c) employment and economy, (d) fire, (e) health, (f) housing and (g) social services. The derivation of the costs and the calculations underpinning these have been quality assured by New Economy in collaboration with the UK government. These costs are useful because they can inform proposals for the implementation of new social interventions as well as measuring and evaluating their impacts.

Tax incentives and superannuation regulation

As noted by Cohen (2020, p. 172), 'the greatest levers at governments' disposal are those that affect the flow of capital from investors'. The UK is one of the first countries to pioneer a specific tax incentive for social investment through the Social Investment Tax Relief (SITR). The SITR was introduced in 2014 and is available to eligible social enterprises, charities and community businesses. It offsets the risk to investors by offering a 30% tax relief on qualifying investments. In Australia, the deductible gift recipient (DGR) rules of the taxation system allow charities with DGR status to receive tax-deductible gifts from donors, but beyond charitable donations, there are no other specific tax incentives for SII.

Government can also affect the flow of capital through regulatory changes to superannuation investing. The superannuation industry in Australia is one of the largest in the world, with close to AUD3 trillion in assets. It represents a potentially vast source of capital for the SII market. However, trustees of superannuation funds may be constrained by current regulatory mandates which can limit significant investments in social impact projects.

Trustees of superannuation funds have a fiduciary responsibility to make investment decisions in the best interests of members as set out in the *Superannuation Industry (Supervision) Act 1993* (the *SIS* Act). Along with general trust law, this fiduciary responsibility is usually interpreted to mean maximising returns to members. Section 52 (para. 6) of the SIS Act also requires a trustee to formulate, review regularly and give effect to an investment strategy, having regard to a range of factors, including risk, return, composition and diversity of investments, liquidity of investments, reliability of valuations, ability to discharge existing and prospective liabilities, expected tax consequences, costs and 'any other relevant matters'.[1]

The Prudential Practice Guide SPG 530 *Investment Governance of the Australian Prudential and Regulatory Authority* (2013) does leave the door open for the superannuation industry to potentially invest in SIIs. Part 34 of *SPG 530* states:

> The SIS Act requires an RSE licensee, when formulating an investment strategy, to give regard to the risk and the likely return from the investments, diversification, liquidity, valuation and other relevant factors. An RSE licensee may take additional factors into account where there is no conflict with the requirements in the SIS Act, including the requirement to act in the best interests of the beneficiaries. This may result in an RSE licensee offering an 'ethical' investment option to beneficiaries to reflect this approach. An 'ethical' investment option is typically characterised by an added focus on environmental, sustainability, social and governance (ESG) considerations, or integrates such considerations into the formulation of the investment strategy and supporting analysis.

According to the guide (SPG 530, para. 35), APRA expects a 'reasoned basis for determining that the investment strategy formulated for such an investment option is in the best interests of beneficiaries, and that it satisfies the requirements of Section 52 of the SIS Act for liquidity and diversification'.

While the SPG 530 clearly allows superannuation investment strategies to actively consider environmental, social and governance (ESG) factors, it does not specifically mention SII. Given the cautionary tone of SPG 530, it is understandable why large superfunds in Australia might interpret the APRA guide conservatively, particularly given the requirements for diversification, liquidity and other considerations in formulating investment strategies under the SIS Act. APRA and government could remove this uncertainty altogether by explicitly encouraging SII as a desirable investment strategy.

Establish a federal ministry for SII

As mentioned in Chapter 5, Cohen (2020, pp. 160–166) recommended appointing a cabinet-level minister to lead social impact policy to ensure that social impact investment is an active part of government policy. While the NSW government has established an Office of Social Impact Investment, a federal government ministry dedicated to SII could boost funding as well as providing more comprehensive strategic policy direction and coordination for SII initiatives across the country. If government is to play an effective role as a market facilitator, a market regulator and as a market participant in the development and growth of the SII market, coordination and oversight of the SII agenda at the highest level of government may prove essential.

The Australian Taskforce on Social Impact Investing is yet to release its final report. We expect the final report will provide more explicit policy detail and strategic direction on how the Australian government intends to support and grow the SII market in Australia – particularly in terms of how SII can be harnessed effectively to address entrenched social problems, how to develop a rigorous approach for measuring and evaluating social impacts, the pros and cons of alternative SII funding approaches (such as SIBs) and how to facilitate greater private capital investment in the Australian SII market.

Key points from Chapter 8

There is a powerful imperative behind SII to fundamentally reshape capitalism and harness the power of capital markets to address entrenched social and environmental challenges such as lack of adequate education and healthcare, homelessness, refugee crises and climate change.

A plethora of different networks and organisations, such as the SASB, GRI, the GIIN and B Lab, have emerged to champion the cause of SII and provide companies, fund managers and other users with robust frameworks and tools to better measure, report and evaluate on social impact.

Various investor surveys sponsored by GIIN, JP Morgan and other organisations have revealed a strong appetite for impact investing across a broad cross section of global investors.

This chapter provides recommendations for government to facilitate the growth of the Australian SII market, in particular (a) facilitate the establishment of an Australian social stock exchange and social investment wholesaler similar to Big Society Capital in the UK; (b) mandating companies to measure and report on their social impacts; (c) government to become a more active purchaser of social outcomes through increased outcome-based contracting or SIB arrangements; (d) improving the quality of data on social outcomes, particularly through the interlinking of various government databases; (e) introducing tax incentives for social investment; (f) providing proactive support for the Australian superannuation industry to be more actively involved in SII; and (g) consideration for creating a federal ministry for SII.

Note

1 A review of the legal ramifications for social impact investing by Australian superannuation funds is provided in Donald et al. (2014).

REFERENCES

ABN-AMRO, 2001, *Does Socially Responsible Equity Portfolios Perform Differently from Conventional Portfolios? If So: How and Why?* ABN-AMRO, Amsterdam, Netherlands.

Addis, R., McKutchan, S., and P. Munro, 2015, *Blueprint to Market: Impact Capital Australia*, Impact Investing Australia, Victoria.

Addis, R., Michaux, F., and S. McKutchan (with contributions from the Australian Advisory Board on Social Impact Investing), 2018, *Scaling Impact: Blueprint for Collective Action to Scale Impact Investment in and from Australia*, Impact Investing Australia, Victoria.

Ahmed, K., 2013, 'Cameron to Push G8 on Finance Bonds for New "Social Investment"', *The Telegraph*, 10 February 2013, viewed 17 November 2020, www.telegraph.co.uk/finance/newsbysector/banksandfinance/9859906/Cameron-to-push-G8-on-finance-bonds-for-new-social-investment.html.

Altman, E., 1968, 'Financial Ratios, Discriminant Analysis and the Prediction of Corporate Bankruptcy', *The Journal of Finance*, 23:4, 589–609.

Al-Tuwaijri, S.A., Christensen, T.E., and K.E. Hughes, 2004, 'The Relations Among Environmental Disclosure, Environmental Performance, and Economic Performance: A Simultaneous Equations Approach', *Accounting, Organizations and Society*, 29:5–6, 447–471.

Andrew, J., and M. Baker, 2020, 'Corporate Social Responsibility Reporting: The Last 40 Years and a Path to Sharing Future Insights', *Abacus*, 56:1, 35–65.

ARTD Consultants, 2020, *Evaluation of the Resilient Families Service, Final Report* (prepared for the NSW Office of Social Impact Investment).

Australian Accounting Standards Board (AASB), 2018, *Conceptual Framework for Financial Reporting*, viewed 19 November 2020, www.aasb.gov.au/admin/file/content102/c3/5.2_PreBallot_CF_M168.pdf.

Australian Charities and Not-for-Profits Commission Act, 2012 (Cwth), viewed 9 November 2020, www.legislation.gov.au/Details/C2012A00168.

Australian Charities and Not-for-Profits Commission (ACNC), 2020a, *Insolvency*, viewed 17 November 2020, www.acnc.gov.au/tools/topic-guides/insolvency.

Australian Charities and Not-for-Profits Commission (ACNC), 2020b, *ACNC Governance Standards*, viewed 17 November 2020, www.acnc.gov.au/for-charities/manage-your-charity/governance-hub/governance-standards.

Australian Ethical Investment, 2020, *Where We Stand*, viewed 17 November 2020, www. australianethical.com.au/personal/ethical-investing/our-positions.

Australian Government (Treasury), 2019, *Australian Government Principles for Social Impact Investing*, viewed 10 November 2020, https://treasury.gov.au/programs-initiatives-consumers-community/social-impact-investing/australian-government-principles-for-social-impact-investing.

Australian Institute of Company Directors, 2019, *The Not-for-Profit Governance Principles* (Second Edition), viewed 10 November 2020, https://aicd.companydirectors.com.au/resources/not-for-profit-resources/not-for-profit-governance-principles.

Australian Prudential and Regulatory Authority (APRA), 2013, *Prudential Practice Guide: SPG 530 Investment Governance*, viewed 13 November 2020, www.apra.gov.au/sites/default/files/prudential-practice-guide-spg-530-investment-governance.pdf.Beck, C., Frost, G., and S. Jones, 2013, *Sustainability Reporting: Practices, Performance and Potential*, CPA Australia, Sydney.

Beck, C., Frost, G., and S. Jones, 2018, 'CSR Disclosure and Financial Performance Revisited: A Cross-Country Analysis', *Australian Journal of Management*, 43:4, 517–537.

Beschorner, T., 2013, 'Creating Shared Value: The One-Trick Pony Approach', *Business Ethics Journal Review*, 1:17, 106–112.

B Lab, 2020a, *About B Lab*, viewed 2 November 2020, https://bcorporation.net/about-b-lab.

B Lab, 2020b, *Certification*, viewed 17 November 2020, https://bcorporation.net/certification.

BlackRock, 2020, *A Fundamental Reshaping of Finance*, viewed 13 November 2020, www. blackrock.com/corporate/investor-relations/larry-fink-ceo-letter.

Blinder, A.S., 2013, *After the Music Stopped: The Financial Crisis, the Response, and the Work Ahead*, Penguin Press, New York.

Bowen, H.R., 1953, *Social Responsibilities of the Businessman*, Harper, New York.

Brandstetter, L., and O.M. Lehner, 2014, *Impact Investment Portfolios: Including Social Risks and Returns*, ACRN Oxford Publishing House, Oxford, UK.

Bugg-Levine, A., and J. Goldstein, 2009, 'Impact Investing: Harnessing Capital Markets to Solve Problems at Scale', *Community Development Investment Review, Federal Reserve Bank of San Francisco*, 2, 30–41.

Burand, D., 2013, 'Globalising Social Finance: How Social Impact Bonds and Social Impact Performance Guarantees can Scale Development', *Journal of Law & Business*, 9, 447–502.

Business Roundtable, 2019, *One Year Later: Purpose of a Corporation: How CEOs Put Principles into Practice*, viewed 22 November 2020, https://purpose.businessroundtable.org/.

Canada's National Advisory Board to the Social Impact Investment Taskforce, 2014, *Mobilizing Private Capital for Public Good: Priorities for Canada*, MaRS, Centre for Impact Investing, Canada.

Carroll, A.B., 1999, 'Corporate Social Responsibility', *Business & Society*, 38:3, 268–295.

Chhichhia, B., 2015, The Rise of Social Stock Exchanges: A New, Innovative Platform Is Helping More Investors Support Social Enterprises, viewed 7 November 2020, https://ssir.org/articles/entry/the_rise_of_social_stock_exchanges#.

Christensen, D.M., Serafeim, G., and A.S. Sikochi, 2021, 'Why Is Corporate Virtue in the Eye of the Beholder? The Case of ESG Ratings (February 26, 2021)', *The Accounting Review*, https://doi.org/10.2308/TAR-2019-0506, Available at SSRN: https://ssrn.com/abstract=3793804.

Clark, G.L., Feiner, A., and M. Viehs, 2015, *From the Stockholder to the Stakeholder: How Sustainability Can Drive Financial Performance*, Smith School of Enterprise and the Environment, University of Oxford and Arabesque Partners.

Clarkson, P.M., Li, Y., Richardson, G.D., and F.P. Vasvari, 2008, 'Revisiting the Relation Between Environmental Performance and Environmental Disclosure: An Empirical Analysis', *Accounting, Organizations and Society*, 33:4–5, 303–327.

Clarkson, P. M., M. B. Overell, and L. Chapple, 2011, 'Environmental Reporting and Its Relation to Corporate Environmental Performance', Abacus, 47(1): 27–60.

Clean Energy Finance Corporation Act 2012, No. 104, 2012.

Cohen, R., 2020, *Impact: Reshaping Capitalism to Drive Real Change*, Ebury Press, London.

Committee for Economic Development, 1971, *Social Responsibilities of Business Corporations. A Statement by the Research and Policy Committee* (1971), View 20 November 2020: https://www.ced.org/pdf/Social_Responsibilities_of_Business_Corporations.pdf

Commonwealth of Australia, Department of the Prime Minister and Cabinet, 2019, Social Impact Investing Taskforce: Interim Report.

Commonwealth of Australia, Department of Treasury, 2014, Financial System Inquiry Financial Report, November 2014.

Crane, A., Palazzo, G., Spence, L.J., and D. Matten, 2014, 'Contesting the Value of "Creating Shared Value"', *California Management Review*, 56:2, 130–153.

Darrat, A.F., Gray, S., Park, J.C., and Y. Wu, 2016, 'Corporate Governance and Bankruptcy Risk', *Journal of Accounting, Auditing and Finance*, 31:2, 163–202.

Davis, K., 1960, 'Can Business Afford to Ignore Social Responsibilities?', California Management Review, 2(3), 1–6.

Del Giudice, A., and M. Migliavacca, 2019, 'Impact Bonds and Institutional Investors: An Empirical Analysis of a Complicated Relationship', *Nonprofit and Voluntary Sector Quarterly*, 48:1, 50–70.

Delmas, V., and C. Burbano, 2011, 'The Drivers of Greenwashing', *California Management Review*, 54:1, 64–87.

Department of the Prime Minister and Cabinet, 2019, *Social Impact Investing Taskforce Interim Report*, viewed 14 November 2020, www.pmc.gov.au/resource-centre/domestic-policy/social-impact-investing-taskforce-interim-report#:~:text=The%20final%20report%2C%20due%20mid,of%20an%20impact%20investing%20wholesaler.

Department of Treasury, 2020, *Australian Government Principles for Social Impact Investing*, viewed 17 November 2020, https://treasury.gov.au/programs-initiatives-consumers-community/social-impact-investing/australian-government-principles-for-social-imp act-investing.

Disley, E., Giacomantonio, C., Kruithof, K., and M. Sim, 2015, *The Payment by Results Social Impact Bond Pilot at HMP Peterborough: Final Process Evaluation Report*, viewed 8 November 2020, www.rand.org/pubs/research_reports/RR1212.html.

Donald, S., Ormiston, J.L., and K. Charlton, 2014, 'The Potential for Superannuation Funds to Make Investments with a Social Impact', *Company and Securities Law Journal*, 32:8, 540–551.

Eccles, R.G., Ioannou, I., and G. Serafeim, 2012, *The Impact of a Corporate Culture of Sustainability on Corporate Behavior and Performance*, viewed 8 November 2020, https://hbswk.hbs.edu/item/the-impact-of-corporate-sustainability-on-organizational-process-and-performance.

Elkington, J., 1997, *Cannibals with Forks: The Triple Bottom Line of 21st Century Business*, Capstone, Oxford.

Emerson, J., 2003, 'The Blended Value Proposition: Integrating Social and Financial Returns', *Californian Management Review*, 45:4, 35–61.

Ernst and Young (EY), 2016, *Social Impact Investing Research, Final Report*, viewed 10 November 2020, www.communitybusinesspartnership.gov.au/wp content/uploads/2016/11/social_impact_investing_research_report.pdf.

Fox, C., and S. Morris, 2021, 'Evaluating Outcome-based Payment Programmes: Challenges for Evidence-based Policy', *Journal of Economic Policy Reform*, 24:1, 61–77.

Fraser, A., Tan, S., Lagarde, M., and N. Mays, 2018, 'Narratives of Promise, Narratives of Caution: A Review of the Literature on Social Impact Bonds', *Social Policy & Administration*, 52:1, 4–28.

Friedman, M., 1970, 'The Social Responsibility of Business Is to Increase Its Profits', *New York Times Magazine*, 13 September, 32:33, 122–126.

Friedman, M., 1982, *Capitalism and Freedom*, University of Chicago Press, Chicago (originally published in 1962).

Freiberg, D., Park, D.G., Serafeim, G., and T.R. Zochowski, 2020, *Corporate Environmental Impact: Measurement, Data and Information*, viewed 10 November 2020, www.hbs.edu/faculty/Pages/item.aspx?num=57938.

Frost, G., Lee, P., and S. Jones, 2013, *Reality and the Rhetoric: Organisational Sustainability Report*, Sydney University Press, Sydney.

Gatti, L., Seele, P., and L. Rademacher, 2019, 'Grey Zone in – Greenwash Out. A Review of Greenwashing Research and Implications for the Voluntary-Mandatory Transition of CSR', *International Journal of Corporate Social Responsibility*, 4:6, 2–15.

Global Impact Investing Network (GIIN), 2019, *Sizing the Impact Investing Market*, viewed 13 November 2020, https://thegiin.org/research/publication/impinv-market-size.

Global Impact Investing Network (GIIN), 2020a, *2020 Annual Impact Investor Survey*, viewed 13 November 2020, https://thegiin.org/research/publication/impinv-survey-2020.

Global Impact Investing Network (GIIN), 2020b, *What Is Impact Investing?* viewed 13 November 2020, https://thegiin.org/impact-investing/need-to-know/#what-is-impact-investing.

Global Impact Investing Network (GIIN), 2020c, *GIIN Goals*, viewed 17 November 2020, https://thegiin.org/giin-goals.

Global Impact Investing Network (GIIN), 2020d, *IRIS+ System*, viewed 17 November 2020, https://iris.thegiin.org/standards.

Global Reporting Initiative (GRI), 2021, A Practical Guide to Sustainability Reporting Using GRI and SASB Standards (published jointly with the Sustainability Accounting Standards Board).

Global Steering Group for Impact Investment (GSG), (2018), *Catalysing an Impact Investment Ecosystem: A Policymaker's Toolkit*, Global Steering Group for Impact Investment, UK.

Goodall, E., 2014, *Choosing Social Impact Bonds: A Practitioner's Guide*, Bridges Ventures, London.

Hulse, E.S.G., Atun, R., and B. McPake, 2021, 'Use of Social Impact Bonds in Financing Health Systems Responses to Non-Communicable Diseases: Scoping Review', *BMJ Global Health*, 6:3, 15.

IDinsight, 2018, *Education Girls Development Impact Bond Final Evaluation Report*, viewed 8 November 2020, https://static1.squarespace.com/static/5b7cc54eec4eb7d25f7af2be/t/5dce708f3c7fd22c0bb30f1a/1573810490043/EG_Final_reduced.pdf.

IIX, 2020, *What We Do*, viewed 17 November 2020, https://iixglobal.com.

Impact Investing Australia, 2016, *Impact Investing Australia 2016 Investor Report*, viewed 17 November 2020, https://impactinvestingaustralia.com/wp-content/uploads/Impact-Investing-Australia-2016-Investor-Report.pdf.

Impact Management Project (IMP), 2020a, *What Is the Impact Management Project?* viewed 19 November 2020, https://impactmanagementproject.com.

Impact Management Project (IMP), 2020b, *Impact Management Norms*, viewed 19 November 2020, https://impactmanagementproject.com/impact-management/impact-management-norms.

iPAR, 2020b, *Impact Framework*, viewed 15 November 2020, https://iparimpact.com/ipar-overview.

IR Magazine, 2019, *More than 100 Companies Using SASB Standards*, viewed 19 November 2020, www.irmagazine.com/reporting/more-100-companies-using-sasb-standards.

Jim, E., and W. John, 1998, 'Small Business Failure and External Risk Factors', *Small Business Economics*, 11:4, 371–390.

Jones, S., 2017, 'Corporate Bankruptcy Prediction: A High Dimensional Analysis', *Review of Accounting Studies*, 22:3, 1366–1422.

Jones, S., and M.E. Aiken, 1994, 'The Significance of the Profit and Loss Account in Nineteenth-Century Britain: A Reassessment', *Abacus*, 30:2, 196–230.

Jones, S., and R.H. Belkaoui, 2010, *Financial Accounting Theory*, Cengage, Sydney.

Jones, S., and G. Frost, 2017, *Sustainability Information and the Cost of Capital – An Australian, United Kingdom and Hong Kong Listed Company Study*, CPA Australia, Victoria.

Jones, S., and D.A. Hensher, 2004, 'Predicting Firm Financial Distress: A Mixed Logit Model', *The Accounting Review*, 79:4, 1011–1038.

Jones, S., and D.A. Hensher, 2007, 'Modelling Corporate Failure: A Multinomial Nested Logit Analysis for Unordered Outcomes', *The British Accounting Review*, 39:1, 89–107.

Jones, S., and D.A. Hensher, 2008, *Advances in Credit Risk Modelling and Corporate Bankruptcy Prediction*, Cambridge University Press, Cambridge, UK.

Jones, S., and R.G. Walker, 2008, 'Local Government in Distress', in Jones, S., and D.A. Hensher (eds), *Advances in Credit Risk Modelling and Corporate Bankruptcy Prediction*, Cambridge University Press, Cambridge, UK, pp. 242–268.

Jones, S., and T. Wang, 2019, 'Predicting Private Company Failure: A Multi-Class Analysis', *Journal of International Financial Markets, Institutions and Money*, 61, 161–188.

Jones, S., and C. Wright, 2018, 'Fashion or Future: Does Creating Shared Value Pay?' *Accounting and Finance*, 58:4, 1111–1139.

Joshua, D., Margolis, J.D., and H.A. Elfenbein, 2008, 'Do Well by Doing Good? Don't Count on It', *Harvard Business Review*, 86:1, 19.

JP Morgan, 2015, *Eyes on the Horizon: The Impact Investor Survey*, JP Morgan, New York.

Kotsantonis, S., and G. Serafeim, 2019, 'Four Things No One Will Tell You About ESG Data', *Journal of Applied Corporate Finance*, 31:2, 50–58.

KPMG, 2017, *The Road Ahead: The KPMG Survey of Corporate Responsibility Reporting 2017*, KPMG International, Amstelveen, Netherlands.

Liebman, J., 2011, *Social Impact Bonds: A Promising New Financing Model to Accelerate Social Innovation and Improve Government Performance*, Center for American Progress, viewed 7 November 2020, https://community-wealth.org/content/social-impact-bonds-promising-new-financial-model-accelerate-social-innovation-and-improve.

Lodhia, S.K., 2012, 'The Need for Effective Corporate Social Responsibility/Sustainability Regulation', in Jones, S., and J. Ratnaunga (eds) *Contemporary Issues in Sustainability Accounting, Assurance and Reporting*, Emerald Group Publishing, Bingley, UK, pp. 139–153.

Mahoney, L.S., Thorne, L.C., and W. LaGore, 2013, 'A Research Note on Standalone Corporate Social Responsibility Reports: Signaling or Greenwashing?' *Critical Perspectives on Accounting*, 24:4–5, 350–359.

Majoch, A.A, Gifford, E.J., and A.G. Hoepner, 2012, 'Active Ownership and ESG Performance', in Jones, S. and J. Ratnaunga (eds) *Contemporary Issues in Sustainability Accounting, Assurance and Reporting*, Emerald Group Publishing, Bingley, UK, pp. 115–139.

Margolis, J.D., and J.P. Walsh, 2003, 'Misery Loves Companies: Rethinking Social Initiatives by Business', *Administrative Science Quarterly*, 48:2, 268–305.

Margolis, J.D., Elfenbein, H.A., and J.P. Walsh, 2007, Does It Pay to be Good? A Meta-analysis and Redirection of Research on the Relationship between Corporate Social and Financial Pperformance, Academy of Management Annual Meeting, Philadelphia, PA.

McClure Report, 2015, *A New System for Better Employment and Social Outcomes (Final Report)*, Commonwealth of Australia, Canberra.

McHugh, N., Sinclair, S., Roy, M., Huckfield, L., and C. Donaldson, 2013, 'Social Impact Bonds: A Wolf in Sheep's Clothing?' *Journal of Poverty and Social Justice*, 21:3, 247–257.

McKinsey Global Institute, 2020, *The Social Contract in the 21st Century: Outcomes So Far for Workers, Consumers, and Savers in Advanced Economies*, viewed 6 November 2020, www.mckinsey.com/industries/public-and-social-sector/our-insights/the-social-contract-in-the-21st-century.

Nestlé, 2010, *Creating Shared Value and Rural Development Summary Report*, viewed 13 November 2020, www.nestle.com/sites/default/files/asset-library/documents/library/documents/corporate_social_responsibility/nestle-csv-summary-report-2010-en.pdf.

New Economy, 2015, *Unit Cost Database*, viewed 19 November 2020, https://golab.bsg.ox.ac.uk/knowledge-bank/resources/unit-cost-database.

New South Wales Office of Social Impact Investment (OSII) 2015, *Social Impact Investment Policy: Leading the Way in Delivering Better Outcomes for the People of NSW*, viewed 13 November 2020, https://www.osii.nsw.gov.au/assets/office-of-social-impact-investm ent/files/Social-Impact-Investment-Policy.pdf.

New South Wales Office of Social Impact Investment (OSII), 2018, *Technical Guide: Outcomes Measurement for Social Impact Investment Proposals to NSW Government*, viewed 13 November 2020, www.osii.nsw.gov.au/assets/office-of-social-impact-investment/Technical-Guide-Outcome-measurement-2018-July.pdf.

OECD, 2019, *Social Impact Investment 2019: The Impact Imperative for Sustainable Development*, OECD Publishing, Paris.

O'Flynn, P., and C. Barnett, 2017, *Evaluation and Impact Investing: A Review of Methodologies to Assess Social Impact*, Institute of Development Studies, Brighton.

Orlitzky, M., Schmidt, F.L., and S.L. Rynes, 2003, 'Corporate Social and Financial Performance: A Meta-Analysis', *Organization Studies*, 24:3, 403–441.

Ormiston, J., Charlton, K., Donald, M.S., and R.G. Seymour, 2015, 'Overcoming the Challenges of Impact Investing: Insights from Leading Investors', *Journal of Social Entrepreneurship*, 6:3, 352–378.

Overland, J., 2007, 'Corporate Social Responsibility in Context: The Case for Compulsory Sustainability Disclosure for Listed Public Companies in Australia?' *Macquarie Journal of International and Comparative Environmental Law*, 4:2, 1–22.

Paramanand, B., 2013, 'Is Porter's Big Idea Yet to Stick', *Management Next*, viewed 10 November 2020, http://managementnext.com/pdf/2013/MN_Jan_2013.pdf.

Porter, M.E., and M.R. Kramer, 2011, 'Creating Shared Value', *Harvard Business Review*, 89:1–2, 62–77.

Porter, M.E., Kramer, M.R., Herman, K., and S. McAra, 2015, *Nestlé's Creating Shared Value Strategy*, viewed 12 November 2020, https://hbsp.harvard.edu/product/716 422-PDF-ENG.

Puttick, R., and J. Ludlow, 2012, *Standards of Evidence for Impact Investing*, viewed 13 November 2020, www.nesta.org.uk/report/standards-of-evidence-for-impact-investing.

PwC report, 2019, ESG in the Boardroom: What Directors Need to Know, Governance Insights Center, viewed 13 November 2020, https://envotherm.dk/wp-content/uplo ads/pwcesgdirectorsboardroom.pdf.

Ramsden, P., 2016, *Social Impact Bonds: State of Play & Lessons Learnt*, OECD Working Paper, viewed 13 November 2020, www.oecd.org/cfe/leed/SIBs-State-Play-Lessons-Final.pdf.

Ratnatunga, J., and S. Jones, 2012, 'A Methodology to Rank the Quality and Comprehensiveness of Sustainability Information Provided in Publicly Listed Company Reports', in Jones, S., and J. Ratnaunga (eds) *Contemporary Issues in Sustainability Accounting, Assurance and Reporting*, Emerald Group Publishing, Bingley, UK, pp. 197–227.

Rockefeller Foundation, 2012, *Unlocking Capital, Activating a Movement: Final Report of the Strategic Assessment of The Rockefeller Foundation's Impact Investing Initiative*, viewed 13 November 2020, www.rockefellerfoundation.org/report/unlocking-capital-activating-a-movement.

Rodin, J., and M. Brandenburg, 2014, *The Power of Impact Investing: Putting Markets to Work for Profit and Global Good*, Wharton Digital Press, Philadelphia.

Roth, B.M., 2019, *Impact Investing: A Theory of Financing Social Entrepreneurship*, viewed 13 November 2020, www.hbs.edu/faculty/Publication%20Files/20-078_8f45e8dc-fbcf-43d9-90fd-d3a6ba59d4c5.pdf.

Sachs, J., Schmidt-Traub, G., Kroll, C., Lafortune, G., Fuller, G., and F. Woelm, 2020, *The Sustainable Development Goals and COVID-19. Sustainable Development Report 2020*, Cambridge University Press, Cambridge.

Saltuk, Y., 2012, *A Portfolio Approach to Impact Investment: A Practical Guide to Building, Analysing and Managing a Portfolio of Impact Investments*, JP Morgan, New York.

Schapire, R., and Y. Freund, 2012, *Boosting: Foundations and Algorithms*, MIT Press, Cambridge, MA.

Serafeim, G., Zochowski, T.R., and J. Downing, 2019, 'Impact Weighted Financial Accounts: The Missing Piece for an Impact Economy', viewed 16 November 2020, www.hbs.edu/impact-weighted-accounts/Documents/Impact-Weighted-Accounts-Report-2019.pdf.

Shinwell, M., and E. Shamir, 2018, *Measuring the Impact of Businesses on People's Wellbeing and Sustainability: Taking Stock of Existing Frameworks and Initiatives*, OECD Statistics Working Papers 2018/08, SDD Working Paper 95.

SIFMA, 2020, *Global Markets Fact Book*, viewed 6 November 2020, www.sifma.org/resources/research/fact-book/.

Smith, N. Craig, 2003, 'Corporate Social Responsibility: Whether or How?' *California Management Review*, 45:4, 52–76.

Social Finance (UK), 2020, *World's First Social Impact Bond to Reduce Reoffending in Peterborough*, viewed 19 November 2020, www.socialfinance.org.uk/peterborough-social-impact-bond.

Social Impact Investment Taskforce, (September 2014), *Impact Investing: The Invisible Heart of Markets: Harnessing the Power of Entrepreneurship, Innovation and Capital for the Public Good*, viewed 7 November 2020, www.socialimpactinvestment.org.

SocialValue International (SVI), 2020, *What Are the Principles of SocialValue?* viewed 19 November 2020, www.socialvalueuk.org/what-is-social-value/the-principles-of-social-value.

Social Value UK, 2012, *A Guide to Social Return on Investment*, viewed 19 November 2020, www.socialvalueuk.org/app/uploads/2016/03/The%20Guide%20to%20Social%20Return%20on%20Investment%202015.pdf.

Social Venture Connexion (SVX), 2020, *Our View on Impact*, viewed 17 November 2020, www.svx.ca/impact.

Social Ventures Australia, 2013, *Information Memorandum: Newpin Social Benefit Bond*, viewed 19 November 2020, www.socialventures.com.au/assets/Newpin-Social-Benefit-Bond-IM-020513.pdf.

South African Social Investment Exchange (SASIX), 2017, *SASIX Research*, viewed 17 November 2020, www.sasix.co.za/sasix-research.

Superannuation Industry (Supervision) Act, 1993 (Cwth), viewed 9 November 2020, www. legislation.gov.au/Details/C2013C00421content/uploads/2019/05/SASB-Conceptual-Framework.pdf.

Sustainability Accounting Standards Board (SASB), 2020a, *Mission*, viewed 17 November 2020, www.sasb.org/governance.

Sustainability Accounting Standards Board (SASB), 2020b, *Why Is Financial Materiality Important?* viewed 17 November 2020, www.sasb.org/standards-overview/materiality-map.

Sustainability Accounting Standards Board (SASB), 2020c, *Sustainability Framework*, viewed 17 November 2020, www.sasb.org/standards-overview/materiality-map/.

Tan, S., Fraser, N., and M.E. Warner, 2019, 'Widening Perspectives on Social Impact Bonds', *Journal of Economic Policy Reform*, 24:1, 1–10.

The International Association for Impact Assessment (IAIA), 2015, *Social Impact Assessment: Guidance for Assessing and Managing the Social Impacts of Projects*, viewed 17 November 2020, www.iaia.org/uploads/pdf/SIA_Guidance_Document_IAIA.pdf.

The International Association for Impact Assessment (IAIA), n.d., *What Is Impact Assessment?* viewed 17 November 2020, www.iaia.org/uploads/pdf/What_is_IA_web.pdf.

The Young Foundation, 2011, *Social Impact Investment: The Challenge and Opportunity of Social Impact Bonds*, viewed 7 November 2020, https://youngfoundation.org/wp-content/uplo ads/2012/10/Social-Impact-Investment-The-opportunity-and-challenge-of-Social-Imp act-Bonds-March-2011.pdf.

Trelstad, B., 2016a, *Making Sense of the Many Kinds of Impact Investing*, viewed 17 November 2020, https://hbr.org/2016/01/making-sense-of-the-many-kinds-of-impact-investing.

Trelstad, B., 2016b, 'Impact Investing: A Brief History', *Capitalism and Society*, 11:2, 1–14.

United Nations (UN), 2020, *Sustainable Development Goals*, viewed 10 November 2020, www.un.org/sustainabledevelopment/sustainable-development-goals.

URBIS, 2018, *Newpin Second Interim Evaluation Report*, viewed 10 November 2020, www. osii.nsw.gov.au/assets/office-of-social-impact-investment/Newpin-Second-Interim-Evaluation-Report-2018-Final.pdf.

Vanclay, F., 2003, 'International Principles for Social Impact Assessment', *Impact Assessment and Project Appraisal*, 21:1, 5–12.

Van Marrewijk, M., 2003, 'Concepts and Definitions of CSR and Corporate Sustainability: Between Agency and Communion', *Journal of Business Ethics*, 44:2/3, 95–105.

Wendt, K., 2020, 'Social Stock Exchanges: Defining the Research Agenda', in La Torre, M., and H. Chiappini (eds) *Contemporary Issues in Sustainable Finance*, Palgrave Studies in Impact Finance, Palgrave Macmillan, Cham.

Yang, Y., and R. Simnett, 2020, 'Financial Reporting by Charities: Why Do Some Choose to Report Under a More Extensive Reporting Framework?' *Abacus*, 56:3, 320–347.

INDEX

Printed in the United States
by Baker & Taylor Publisher Services